Anne Hathaway

Other books in the People in the News series:

Anne Hathaway

Cherese Cartlidge

LUCENT BOOKS
A part of Gale, Cengage Learning

GALE
CENGAGE Learning·

Detroit • New York • San Francisco • New Haven, Conn • Waterville, Maine • London

Library of Congress Cataloging-in-Publication Data

Cartlidge, Cherese.
Anne Hathaway / by Cherese Cartlidge.
     p. cm. -- (People in the news)
Includes bibliographical references and index.
ISBN 978-1-4205-0751-5 (hardcover)
1. Hathaway, Anne, 1982---Juvenile literature. 2. Motion picture actors and actresses--United States--Biography--Juvenile literature. 3. Actresses--United States--Biography--Juvenile literature. I. Title.
PN2287.H325C37 2013
791.45'028'092--dc23
[B]

2012047680

Lucent Books
27500 Drake Rd
Farmington Hills MI 48331

ISBN-13: 978-1-4205-0751-5
ISBN-10: 1-4205-0751-6

Printed in the United States of America
1 2 3 4 5 6 7 17 16 15 14 13

Contents

Fame and celebrity are alluring. People are drawn to those who walk in fame's spotlight, whether they are known for great accomplishments or for notorious deeds. The lives of the famous pique public interest and attract attention, perhaps because their experiences seem in some ways so different from, yet in other ways so similar to, our own.

Newspapers, magazines, and television regularly capitalize on this fascination with celebrity by running profiles of famous people. For example, television programs such as *Entertainment Tonight* devote all their programming to stories about entertainment and entertainers. Magazines such as *People* fill their pages with stories of the private lives of famous people. Even newspapers, newsmagazines, and television news frequently delve into the lives of well-known personalities. Despite the number of articles and programs, few provide more than a superficial glimpse at their subjects.

Lucent's People in the News series offers young readers a deeper look into the lives of today's newsmakers, the influences that have shaped them, and the impact they have had in their fields of endeavor and on other people's lives. The subjects of the series hail from many disciplines and walks of life. They include authors, musicians, athletes, political leaders, entertainers, entrepreneurs, and others who have made a mark on modern life and who, in many cases, will continue to do so for years to come.

These biographies are more than factual chronicles. Each book emphasizes the contributions, accomplishments, or deeds that have brought fame or notoriety to the individual and shows how that person has influenced modern life. Authors portray their subjects in a realistic, unsentimental light. For example, Bill Gates—cofounder of the software giant Microsoft—has been instrumental in making personal computers the most vital tool of the modern age. Few dispute his business savvy, his perseverance, or his technical expertise, yet critics say he is ruthless in his dealings with competitors and driven more by his desire to maintain Microsoft's dominance in the computer industry than by an interest in furthering technology.

In these books, young readers will encounter inspiring stories about real people who achieved success despite enormous obstacles. Oprah Winfrey—one of the most powerful, most watched, and wealthiest women in television history—spent the first six years of her life in the care of her grandparents while her unwed mother sought work and a better life elsewhere. Her adolescence was colored by pregnancy at age fourteen, rape, and sexual abuse.

Each author documents and supports his or her work with an array of primary and secondary source quotations taken from diaries, letters, speeches, and interviews. All quotes are footnoted to show readers exactly how and where biographers derive their information and provide guidance for further research. The quotations enliven the text by giving readers eyewitness views of the life and accomplishments of each person covered in the People in the News series.

In addition, each book in the series includes photographs, annotated bibliographies, timelines, and comprehensive indexes. For both the casual reader and the student researcher, the People in the News series offers insight into the lives of today's newsmakers—people who shape the way we live, work, and play in the modern age.

The Real Deal

Anne Hathaway's name has been on people's lips ever since she first appeared before audiences in the 2001 Disney hit movie *The Princess Diaries*. Since then, her career trajectory has been solid, with Hathaway appearing in some of the most talked-about movies of the new century, including *Brokeback Mountain* (2005), *The Devil Wears Prada* (2006), and *Alice in Wonderland* (2010). She has held her own on-screen with several big-name stars, among them Julie Andrews and Meryl Streep. She has even been nominated for an Academy Award for best actress, for her performance in *Rachel Getting Married* (2008). Directors and producers know she is one of the most bankable actors around today, with her films consistently doing well at the box office and with movie reviewers.

Girl Next Door

Hathaway, who became an overnight success at age eighteen with *The Princess Diaries*, had a meteoric career rise, appearing in fifteen films by the time she was twenty-five. In addition to her obvious talent as an actor, one of the things that makes Hathaway such a hit with audiences is Hathaway herself. She has a genuineness that brings depth to her acting and resonates with viewers. What viewers see is what they get: Hathaway is the real deal, as honest on-screen as she is off. "If I'm not true to myself, there's no way that I'm gonna be able to do my job," she says. "I don't know anything about playing games. I'm kind of a Labrador puppy of a person, it's all out there, wearing my heart on my sleeve, that whole thing."[1]

Hathaway has built her stardom on her ability to combine her talent, grace, and intelligence with girl-next-door appeal.

A writer for *Vogue* magazine noted that Hathaway "feels like a girl you might actually know."[2] Audiences identify with her because she seems like a real person when she is on-screen, like the proverbial girl next door. She is beautiful in a wholesome way, with porcelain skin, doe eyes, an alluring smile, and a thick mane of chestnut hair. She is willowy, graceful, and tall; she stands five feet eight inches and frequently wears heels that push her height up to six feet. Hathaway has a habit of waving her long arms dramatically in the air when she talks, which is often. She has a bubbly personality and is very talkative and energetic in person.

She is also intelligent and has a quick wit. For all her beauty, intelligence, and success, however, she remains humble and modest. Her fame seems not to have affected the honest, earnest young woman whom audiences first glimpsed as an adolescent. One interviewer described her as "unguarded" and noted, "She takes long, confident strides in downtown New York, seemingly oblivious to her own celebrity."[3]

"Classic Cinema Magic"

Of course, Hathaway's success is also due to her undeniable talent. She can act, sing, dance, and has a good sense of humor. She possesses the grace and charm of iconic actresses of the past, such as Judy Garland and Audrey Hepburn, and is also frequently compared with a more contemporary actress, Julia Roberts—all of them personal idols of hers. Lone Scherfig, who directed Hathaway in the 2011 film *One Day*, describes her talent as "classic cinema magic that happens in front of your eyes."[4]

Hathaway is very versatile as an actress, something that led to her being chosen as Harvard University's Hasty Pudding Theatricals' 2010 Woman of the Year. Said David J. Smolinsky, a spokesperson for the theatrical organization, "What impressed us the most has definitely been her range and the ability with which she can play such diverse characters."[5] He cited her roles in films that ranged from comedies such as *Get Smart* (2008) to more serious films like *The Devil Wears Prada* and *Brokeback Mountain*.

In addition to playing a variety of characters, Hathaway has also tackled several different genres. Her works include light-hearted family fare, serious drama, romantic comedy, satire, and even slapstick humor in *Bride Wars* (2009). She has also appeared in historical films, including *Becoming Jane* (2007), in which she played nineteenth-century English novelist Jane Austen. And she has ventured into different mediums, as well, including narrating audiobooks, doing voice-overs in animated TV shows and films, and even appearing onstage in New York, performing in musical theater and Shakespeare. Meryl Streep, who is quick to heap praise on her *Prada* costar, beams, "She is the kind of actor who can do all sorts of things."[6]

Devoted to Acting

Hathaway is extremely dedicated to her chosen profession. She grew up watching her mother, Kate McCauley, perform in regional theater and fell in love with the stage. She began studying acting at the tender age of ten and went on to become the youngest person ever admitted to Manhattan's Barrow Group Theater Company. Today, she literally breathes acting. "I wake up in the morning," she says, "and the first breath I take is in the devotion of acting."[7]

That devotion to acting can be seen not only on-screen but in the way she conducts herself in her personal life as well. Hathaway has managed to avoid the drinking, drugging, and other sensational scandals that plague other young celebrities today. With one notable exception—the arrest of former boyfriend Raffaello Follieri for fraudulent activities, in which Hathaway had no part—she has kept her name out of scandalous headlines. No examples of wild partying, public meltdowns, or deep, dark secrets grace the covers of supermarket tabloids. "I'm a boring person, really,"[8] she laughs.

Hathaway stays grounded in her turbulent profession by remembering what drew her to acting in the first place. Hathaway claims she did not pursue acting for the fame; rather, she is motivated by a genuine love of her craft. Because of this dedication, she does her best to keep her personal life private and maintain a low profile with the paparazzi. "I try to stay out of the spotlight as much as humanly possible," she explains, "because I think that when actors . . . are living very public lives, it affects your ability to get lost in their performances."[9]

Thanks to her sincerity on-screen and off, the multitalented Hathaway will likely continue producing cinema magic, and audiences will likely be getting lost in her performances for a long time to come.

Chapter 1

The World of Pretend

Anne Jacqueline Hathaway was born on November 12, 1982, in Brooklyn, New York. Her parents, Gerald Hathaway and Kate McCauley, may have had an inkling that their daughter would one day become a critically acclaimed actress. After all, they gave her a name that is associated with the theater: She is named after Anne Hathaway, the wife of William Shakespeare. The choice of their daughter's name was likely influenced by Kate's own background as a stage actress.

Anne's father, Gerald, earned a law degree from the University of Pittsburgh School of Law. He was a lawyer when Anne was growing up, and he still works as a lawyer today. When Anne was a child, her father made her promise never to lie to anyone. He also made her promise never to ride a motorcycle and not to get a tattoo until she was an adult (today she sports a small tattoo of the letter *M* on the inside of her left wrist). Thanks to her father's prestigious job and her mother's second income as an actress, Anne enjoyed an upper-middle-class childhood.

Anne is Gerald and Kate's second of three children. She has an older brother, Michael, and a younger brother, Thomas. She and her two brothers got along well and were very close to each other as children. Her family called her Annie when she was a child (an affectionate name that her family and close friends still use for her today). As the only girl growing up with two brothers, Anne was a bit of a tomboy, engaging in rough-and-tumble games outside with her brothers, including playing soldier. She also played soccer all through childhood and into adolescence.

A Bright and Independent Girl

Anne's parents raised her and her brothers Roman Catholic and instilled strong morals and values in their children. Anne attended preschool at Brooklyn Heights Montessori School, where she joined the other kids in a mixed-age classroom. She was a bright and creative child, and enjoyed the wide range of learning activities the students were allowed to choose from, including painting, arts and crafts, story time, musical activities, and exploring mathematical concepts. The school, with its emphasis on independent learning, was an especially good fit for Anne because of the self-sufficiency she showed from a young age.

Anne attended the Montessori school for only one year. In 1988 her family moved to Millburn, New Jersey. Anne grew up in this small town roughly 20 miles (32km) east of Brooklyn. Although technically she was not old enough to enter the first

Hathaway's parents, Kate McCauley, left, and Gerald Hathaway raised Anne and her two brothers in Millburn, New Jersey.

grade yet, since her sixth birthday was not until November, Anne was already intellectually and emotionally mature enough to start school. She was allowed to enroll that fall in first grade at the Wyoming Elementary School in Millburn. She was a good student and earned good grades in elementary school and, later, at Millburn Middle School.

Anne was an intelligent child who loved to be read to and, later, to read on her own. Among her favorite stories were the Hans Christian Andersen fairy tale *The Snow Queen* and the Brothers Grimm fairy tale *The Fisherman and His Wife*. In fact, she liked the latter so much that her parents bought her a copy of the book *Grimms' Fairy Tales* when she was a child, despite the often gruesome themes of the stories. The book of fairy tales quickly became her favorite. "I used to stay up late reading them to myself," she says. "Because they are really violent, they're kind of fabulous."[10]

"In a Different World"

Anne had a vivid imagination, which her voracious appetite for reading helped nurture. She adored being drawn into the world of fairy tales and novels, in large part because she was especially attracted to the world of pretend. As many kids do, she liked to play dress-up and make-believe. "For as long as I can remember, I've always played make-believe,"[11] she says. Anne always went a step further with her make-believe games, however, and felt as if she actually became whatever she was pretending to be. "If we were playing a war game," she explains, "all of a sudden I was on a battlefield. You couldn't tell me I wasn't." She says it was as if she were "in a different world."[12]

She credits this degree of immersion in her games of pretend with the fact that acting is in her blood. Watching her mother act onstage was a huge influence on young Anne. Among other notable roles, Kate played Fantine in the first national tour of the musical *Les Misérables* in 1987, when Anne was four years old. As a child, Anne also watched her mother perform the role of Argentinean First Lady Eva Perón in a regional production of *Evita*.

Watching her actress mother, Kate McCauley, right, perform on stage influenced Anne's decision to become an actress herself when she was a young girl.

Joe McCauley

Kate McCauley, Anne Hathaway's mother, is not Anne's only relative to work in show business. Kate's father and Anne's grandfather, Joe McCauley, was one of Philadelphia's most popular radio personalities from the 1930s through the 1960s. A native of South Philadelphia, McCauley graduated from La Salle High School in 1937. As class valedictorian, he had done some public speaking during high school and decided he wanted to work in radio. During an interview conducted in the last year of his life, McCauley explained that he got his first job in radio immediately after graduation, at WHAT Radio, a small, independent station in Philadelphia. "I was fortunate," he said. "I walked into WHAT to just ask for a summer job. And the program director . . . decided that maybe I could be helpful, hanging around, doing little odd jobs. And they had no money to pay me; they said they would give me car fare and lunch money, if I wanted to work for that."

After two weeks, a full-time paid job opened up for him at the station; that fall he decided to stay with the job rather than attend college. Starting in 1942, McCauley hosted an all-night program for Philadelphia's WIP Radio called *The Dawn Patrol*. In 1954 he moved to WIP's morning show, which he hosted until his death in 1968. For his contribution to radio, he was inducted into the Broadcast Pioneers of Philadelphia Hall of Fame in 1999.

Joe McCauley, interviewed by Florence Weiss. *In & Around*. WRTI-FM, Monday, April 24, 1967.

It was from watching her mother onstage that Anne first began to develop the idea of becoming an actress herself one day. Anne later said of her mother, "She's the one that taught me it was a possibility."[13] In addition to her mother, Anne was also influenced by old movies on TV. She particularly enjoyed watching anything that featured Judy Garland, who played Dorothy in the 1939 classic *The Wizard of Oz*, or Audrey Hepburn, another idol of hers. Growing up,

Anne also adored the immensely talented Meryl Streep. She says, "Watching Meryl Streep in [the 1982 film] *Sophie's Choice* I'm like, 'OK, I want to do that, I definitely want to do that.'"[14]

Big Changes for Anne

Young Anne considered a few other career ideas, including teacher, orthopedic surgeon, and even president, but these were all passing fancies. There was, however, one other profession the Catholic-raised Anne considered: being a nun. When she was

Hathaway is accompanied by her brothers Tom, left, and Michael at an Empire State Pride Agenda event in 2009. She speaks proudly of her family's acceptance of Michael, who is gay, and she has been an advocate for many LGBT causes.

around eleven years old, she believed that God was asking her to become a nun, and for several years she thought it was her destiny to join a convent. "I felt like I got a calling from God,"[15] she explains.

By the time Anne was fifteen, however, her religious views were deeply challenged following a serious revelation from her older brother, Michael. He told his family and closest friends that he was gay. Anne recalls, "When my brother came out, we hugged him, said we loved him, and that was that."[16]

The entire Hathaway family was very accepting of Michael's homosexuality. The Catholic Church, however, views homosexuality as a sin, which is something Anne could not accept. She realized she could not support a religion that condemned her brother for being gay. She began to reexamine her religious beliefs, beginning with rejecting the idea of becoming a nun. She also turned away from Catholicism entirely; in fact, her whole family converted to Episcopalianism. As Anne went through her later teenage years, she began to consider herself as a nondenominational Christian—meaning that she was a Christian but did not embrace any one particular sect of Christianity.

There were other changes for Anne during her teenage years. Like many adolescents, she went through a period of rebelliousness, talking back to her parents and teachers and sometimes getting into trouble for breaking simple rules such as curfews. "If I disagreed with something, I was always encouraged to argue my stance," she recalls, "and even if I lost, I would usually go off and do my own thing anyway."[17] She admits that she was "a bit of a brat and probably rather rebellious just for the sake of being rebellious."[18]

"Acting Was an Escape"

Once being a nun was off the table, Anne followed in her mother's footsteps and began acting. Starting at age ten, she began appearing onstage in several productions at Millburn's regional theater, the Paper Mill Playhouse. The theater school director there,

Mickey McNany, noticed her natural self-confidence onstage and cast her in productions of *Gigi* and *Aladdin*.

While preparing for *Aladdin*, Anne's creativity and commitment to the stage came through in the preteen's costume. During the dress rehearsal, she spontaneously grabbed a piece of fabric that was lying around and added a sash to her dress, then used another piece of extra fabric to create a headpiece for herself. This imagination and initiative impressed the director, McNany, who recalls, "Even at such a young age she showed tremendous focus and a love of performing that would inspire everyone else in the cast."[19]

In the beginning, acting for Anne was as an extension of her earlier fondness for playing make-believe. "When I first started out," she recalls, "acting was an escape."[20] But it did not take long for her to realize that, for her, there was more to acting than just escaping into another world. She began to enjoy acting for its own sake and loved performing onstage.

Anne continued to appear in plays at the Paper Mill Playhouse, as well as in school productions, throughout middle school and high school. She appeared in school productions of *Meet Me in St. Louis* and *Oliver!* She also studied at the Paper Mill Playhouse's Summer Musical Theatre Conservatory program beginning when she was in middle school. She managed to keep her grades up even while rehearsing, performing, and studying acting. She attended Millburn High School, where she was an A student, except for slightly lower grades in mathematics.

"How Come I'm Not in New York?"

Anne took another step toward a career in acting when she started auditioning for TV commercials. She landed her first commercial at age fourteen for Better Homes and Gardens Real Estate. In the commercial, she says good-bye to her boyfriend, who is moving away, by tearfully throwing her arms around him and whispering that she will miss him.

Other commercials followed, including a regional commercial for Cincinnati Bell when she was fifteen. She was gaining valuable experience by appearing in commercials, but Anne did not really like making them. As she describes it, she would "take a train, go into the city and smile for a Cheez Whiz commercial."[21] Neither excited nor fulfilled by the experience of making commercials, she wanted more.

Her dissatisfaction with appearing in commercials was not the only problem Anne faced at the beginning of her acting career. The stress of going on auditions and the rejections she inevitably sometimes encountered began to take a toll on her emotional well-being. She started to experience frequent bouts of anxiety as a teenager and sank into a depression.

Looking back on this time in her life, she believes she was too self-absorbed and had trouble keeping things in perspective, which contributed to her feeling depressed. For example, she became hung up on the fact that she lived in New Jersey instead of New York. "The town I grew up in is beautiful," she said in a 2011 interview. "But it's not a place I wanted to stay. . . . My feeling about growing up in New Jersey was, 'How come I'm not in New York?'"[22]

Anne, who expected a lot from herself, recalls an emotional meltdown she had one day when she was sixteen. "I remember sobbing in the kitchen and my mom said: 'What's the matter?' I said: 'Tara Lipinski won a gold medal at 15 [in figure skating at the 1998 Winter Olympics]. I am now 16. What do I have to show for it?'"[23]

Rather than take medication to help lift her mood, Anne worked through her depression in a variety of ways. Although she had turned away from the Catholic Church, her faith was still very strong. She also talked to her parents, who helped her realize that the kind of pressure she was putting on herself was not healthy for anyone, especially for someone so young. She remembers that when she would get a rejection, her parents would tell her, "You can give this up at any time. It is your choice. You are choosing to do this, you're not required to do anything."[24] Her parents suggested she might be taking things too seriously, and she realized they were right. Anne learned to lighten up on herself, and felt more free and happy.

A Rising Star

Now that she had learned to better handle life's everyday anxieties as well as the rejections that often come with acting, Anne was able to approach her craft in a healthier way. She threw herself into acting with passion, although she was still determined to be the best. As a close friend of hers said several years later, "She was the girl who, in high school, probably ran up to the bulletin board, pushing the other girls out of the way, to be the first one to look at the casting list."[25]

One time she found her name on the list for a play that would become another stepping stone for her. In 1998 she appeared

Hathaway's performances in productions at her New Jersey high school and other acting work as a teenager earned her the attention of theater groups in New York City as well as several prestigious honors.

The Paper Mill Playhouse

The Paper Mill Playhouse was founded in 1934 on the site of a former paper mill, the Diamond Mill Paper Company. The theater's first performance came four years later, with a production of *The Kingdom of God* by Spanish playwright Gregorio Martinez Sierra. Throughout the next several decades, the theater continued to feature a variety of classic and modern plays, as well as operettas. But after a fire damaged part of the building in 1980, the Paper Mill Playhouse was forced to close for renovation. It reopened on October 30, 1982, just two weeks before Anne Hathaway was born in nearby Brooklyn, New York.

The Paper Mill Playhouse is notable as a pioneer in the American regional theater movement. Regional theaters are professional or semiprofessional theater companies outside of New York City that organize and sponsor their own productions, often of new plays that may not have enough commercial appeal for Broadway. Today the twelve-hundred-seat Paper Mill Playhouse is one of the most acclaimed nonprofit professional theaters in the United States. In 1972 the governor designated it as the official state theater of New Jersey. Since 1971 the New Jersey Ballet has been the resident ballet company of the Paper Mill Playhouse, where it puts on an annual production of Tchaikovsky's *The Nutcracker*.

in a school production of *Once upon a Mattress*, in which she played a princess opposite fellow Millburn High student Jeffrey Seelbach. For her performance, Anne was nominated for a Rising Star Award, which is given annually by the Paper Mill Playhouse to the top performers in New Jersey high school musicals.

The nomination helped Anne gain positive attention. Soon after appearing in *Once upon a Mattress*, she began to study acting with the Barrow Group Theater Company in Manhattan. She was the youngest person, and the only teenager, ever accepted into the award-winning Barrow Group's acting program. She studied with the Barrow Group for six months.

In addition to acting, Anne also enjoyed singing. A soprano, she studied with several voice coaches as a teen and joined various choral groups in Millburn. When she was sixteen, Anne performed in two concerts as a member of the All-Eastern United States High School Honors Chorus at Carnegie Hall in New York City. Performing at such a prestigious venue was a thrilling moment for the teenager, yet she knew it was not what she really wanted to do.

Anne had always aspired to be a stage actress. "Maybe I could make it onto Broadway," she says, describing her goals at this stage in her life, "and if I found the right role in the right year maybe get nominated for a Tony [Award]. That was kind of the extent of my dreams."[26] But despite her accomplishments thus far, she had doubts she would make it as an actress.

Getting Real

Three days after performing at Carnegie Hall, Anne decided to take a chance on herself by trying something that was a little different for her: She auditioned for a part in a Fox Network series called *Get Real*. To her surprise and delight, she won the role of high-schooler Meghan Green on the comedy-drama. Anne left New Jersey and went to Los Angeles to begin filming the show. Because she was only sixteen, her mother accompanied her.

The show featured a San Francisco family, the Greens. Anne and costar Eric Christian Olsen played the two oldest children in the family, and Jesse Eisenberg played the youngest child. Anne knew the show was her big break, and she was thrilled to be on it. She was gaining much professional experience in her field, as well as getting her name and face before the public. Playing Meghan was a real education for her and provided her with many firsts; for example, her first screen kiss, at age sixteen, was on *Get Real*. "I was so scared I was shaking for like two weeks beforehand,"[27] she recalls.

Get Real ran for one season, from September 1999 to April 2000. Twenty-two hour-long episodes were filmed, but the last two episodes never aired. Anne's work on the series earned her a

Hathaway, third from left, was cast in Fox's family comedy-drama Get Real *in 1999, along with costars, from left, Debrah Farentino, Jon Tenney, Christina Pickles, Jesse Eisenberg, and Eric Olsen.*

nomination for a Teen Choice Award for Best Actress in a Drama, however. Also, even though the series was canceled after only a year, her exposure to a national audience had put her solidly in the minds of several Hollywood producers and casting directors. By the time Anne graduated from Millburn High School at age seventeen in 2000, she was already on her way to a promising career as an actress and her career was about to take a big leap forward.

Hollywood Princess

As the new century dawned, Anne Hathaway's career as an actress took off. Her first movie role led to an unexpected opportunity that would pay off big for her. Thanks to her success early in her film career, she became a role model for children and, especially, young women. Yet Hathaway's personal doubts over her own abilities as an actress persisted as she went through college. At one point, fearing she would be typecast forever in the same type of role, she debated giving up acting altogether.

A Chance Audition

As she neared her high school graduation in the spring of 2000, the seventeen-year-old Hathaway landed her first role in a motion picture, *The Other Side of Heaven*. In this Disney movie, she plays the girlfriend of a Mormon missionary, with whom she corresponds by letter while he is on a three-year-long mission in the South Pacific in the 1950s. The movie, which was based on the memoirs of John H. Groberg, was filmed entirely in New Zealand.

Hathaway was very excited about being cast in her first movie while still in high school. This was her chance to show off her talent as an actress, and she hoped it would be her big break. There was one unfortunate incident during the production of the movie, however. While filming the opening scene, in which Hathaway and her costar, Christopher Gorham, dance together at a college dance, she was accidentally kicked in the head by

Hathaway played the girlfriend of a Mormon missionary in the 2001 film The Other Side of Heaven, *her first movie role.*

one of the other actors and was knocked to the ground, nearly losing consciousness.

Although *The Other Side of Heaven* would not turn out to be the big break she had hoped for, being cast in this movie did lead Hathaway down a path toward bigger and better things. While she was on her way to the set in New Zealand, she made a stop in Los Angeles to audition for a part in another Disney film, *The Princess Diaries*. This movie was based on the best-selling book of the same name by Meg Cabot, and Hathaway hoped to land the lead. At the end of her audition, something happened that helped her clinch the part: She was so excited that she lost her balance and fell off her chair. This bit of humorous clumsiness was just what the film's director, Garry Marshall, had in mind for the movie's klutzy princess. After only one audition, Hathaway was chosen over hundreds of other girls for the part.

Hathaway was in her hotel room in New Zealand one rainy day when she got the phone call from her agent telling her she had landed the part. She recalls her reaction to the news: "I just screamed, I jumped on my bed. My brother was with me and I went and I hugged him. . . . I said, 'Oh my God, oh my God, I'm so happy. I need to call my mother.'" She remembers that moment as "one of the happier moments of my life. It was truly, truly great."[28]

Although *The Other Side of Heaven* was actually filmed first, Disney delayed its release until after that of *The Princess Diaries*. Studio executives and producers believed that *The Princess Diaries* would be a hit, and they hoped the success of that movie would help ticket sales of *The Other Side of Heaven*.

"Hollywood Royalty"

As soon as she finished filming her scenes for *The Other Side of Heaven*, Hathaway dove straight into her next project, *The Princess Diaries*. She plays the part of Mia Thermopolis, a smart but klutzy American schoolgirl who discovers that she is actually the princess of Genovia, a fictitious European country. The part of her grandmother is played by screen icon Julie Andrews, who

Klutzy Annie

Anne Hathaway won the role of the klutzy Mia Thermopolis in *The Princess Diaries* when she fell off her chair at her audition. This clumsy streak of hers continued through the making of *The Princess Diaries 2*. She reveals a mishap that occurred one day on the set of that film: "I was walking down the stairs to my trailer and fell down the stairs, was caught by the back of my dress and was literally hanging by the back of my dress on a railing! It was really embarrassing!"

Hathaway has quite a reputation for being clumsy, and so the cast and crew of *The Princess Diaries 2* was rightfully nervous when it came time to film the movie's opening scene, in which Hathaway had to shoot flaming arrows. "Fortunately," she says, "I had professionals with me at all times who kept me from getting on fire."

Quoted in It's My Life. "Anne Hathaway." PBS Kids. http://pbskids.org/itsmylife/celebs/interviews/anne.html.

played the title role in *Mary Poppins* (1964) and starred in the 1965 classic *The Sound of Music*. Hathaway, who loved working with Andrews on *The Princess Diaries*, says, "She's just fantastic, she's royalty, a lady with a capital L. She knows how to make people laugh. . . . She's completely gracious, and so witty and funny, and her great ideas always make a scene better."[29]

Hathaway says that she and her character, Mia, have something in common: "We're both absolute complete 100% klutzes."[30] Perhaps it was Hathaway's ability to make Mia seem so real that helped make *The Princess Diaries* such a big hit with audiences; the movie grossed $165 million worldwide. Hathaway gained widespread recognition and praise for her breakout film. Ben Falk of the BBC wrote that she "shines in the title role, and generates great chemistry with her legendary British mentor [Andrews]."[31] Hathaway was nominated again for a Teen Choice Award for

Hathaway played a klutzy teen turned royal heir opposite Julie Andrews, left, in **The Princess Diaries** *in 2001, her breakout film.*

her work on the film, as well as an MTV Movie Award for Best Breakthrough Performance.

This movie made her an overnight star before her nineteenth birthday and turned her into what one writer for *Vogue* magazine called "Hollywood royalty."[32] But even Hathaway's newfound fame could not save *The Other Side of Heaven* at the box office when it was released; it performed poorly and got mostly negative reviews. The success of *The Princess Diaries*, however, led Hathaway to receive a lot of attention from the media and the public. *People* magazine put her on its list of the 25 Most Intriguing People of 2001, and *Teen People* magazine listed her as one of the Hottest Stars Under 25. She made guest appearances on ABC's *Politically Incorrect* and MTV's *Total Request Live*. Meanwhile, fan websites began to appear on the Internet. And, most importantly, the movie offers began pouring in. Hathaway had achieved fame and recognition as an actress. Her career was already soaring and she was still in her teens. She was, as she said in a 2002 interview, "about as lucky as you can be at 19."[33]

A Princess Again

Hathaway played another princess in *Ella Enchanted* (2004), the film version of the book by Gail Carson Levine. Her character, Ella, has been put under a spell that forces her to do everything anybody tells her to do whether she wants to or not. Hathaway, who had read the book when she was sixteen, was thrilled when the opportunity to play the part arose. Always a voracious reader, after talking with the book's author during the production of the film, Hathaway even toyed briefly with the idea of becoming a children's book author.

Preparing to play Ella involved rigorous training, because the part was very physical. Always athletic, Hathaway trained with a kick-boxing instructor for a month and spent two weeks working with a mime. She also worked with a choreographer to prepare for the dance sequences. It was very demanding work, but Hathaway enjoyed every minute of it. She had a lot of fun making the romantic comedy and says, "The thing that I love about it was it makes fun of itself for being a fairy tale."[34]

The tongue-in-cheek humor of *Ella Enchanted* made it a big hit with audiences and movie reviewers alike. Film critic Roger Ebert commented, "One of the charms of the movie is its goofiness." He

Hathaway was once again played a princess in the 2004 film Ella Enchanted *opposite Hugh Dancy, right.*

called Hathaway "luminous" with her "big smile and open face" and said, "The look of the movie is delightful. . . . This is the best family film so far this year."[35]

A Role Model

Hathaway followed up the success of *Ella Enchanted* by returning to the role of Mia Thermopolis for the film *The Princess Diaries 2: Royal Engagement*. At first she was hesitant about making the movie because she was afraid of being typecast in princess-like roles in wholesome, family movies. She was also nervous about making a sequel; oftentimes, sequels are not as good as the original, and she did not want to detract from the original *Princess Diaries* movie by appearing to be capitalizing on its popularity and success. She credits the film's director, Garry Marshall, with reassuring her that the film, and her career, would turn

From One Princess to Another

In *The Princess Diaries* movies, Academy Award–winning British actress Julie Andrews plays the part of Mia's grandmother, who grooms the awkward young Mia by giving her a makeover and teaching her to walk and talk like a princess. The choice of Andrews for this role was especially appropriate because she had played Eliza Dolittle in the 1956 Broadway musical *My Fair Lady*, in which Eliza is similarly transformed by a mentor who teaches her how to walk and talk like an aristocrat.

There are other similarities in the early careers of Hathaway and Andrews. After appearing on Broadway as Eliza Dolittle, Andrews went on to play a princess in the Rodgers and Hammerstein TV musical *Cinderella* on CBS in 1957. This and her sugary-sweet roles in the films *Mary Poppins* and *The Sound of Music* led to Andrews's being typecast. Audiences had trouble accepting her in other types of roles, and her career suffered as a result. Hathaway, who was well aware of the phenomenon of being typecast and was eager to avoid having the same thing happen to her, took Andrews's experience to heart. "By the end of *Princess Diaries 2*," says Hathaway, "I was ready to do something completely different."

Quoted in iVillage. "Anne Hathaway Interview." www.ivillage.co.uk/anne-hathaway-interview/80315?field_pages=0.

out fine. Ultimately, what convinced her to do the movie was when Marshall sat her down and said, "Do you understand how happy this will make people, like little girls across the world?"[36] Hathaway knew that many of her young fans were eagerly hoping for a sequel to *The Princess Diaries*, and she did not want to disappoint them by refusing to make one.

Movie reviewers generally found *The Princess Diaries 2* to be bland and predictable, but that did not stop young fans from

Hathaway signs autographs at the premiere of **The Princess Diaries 2: Royal Engagement** *in 2004. Her role in the Disney-produced* **Princess Diaries** *movies earned her many young fans.*

flocking to see it. The box-office success of *Princess Diaries 2* (in which Hathaway's mother had a small part as the choir director) helped make Hathaway a bona fide movie star.

Yet there was more to her than being a big star. Having played a princess in three successive hit movies gave her a reputation for playing this kind of role. And her doe-eyed innocence helped make her a tween icon and a role model for young women. She was adored by teen girls and their mothers, who saw her as a wholesome role model for their young daughters. Tommy O'Haver, the director of *Ella Enchanted*, summed up Hathaway's appeal by saying she possessed a "mixture of child-like purity but also the confidence and smarts of a mature young woman."[37]

Hathaway was proud to have touched so many people's hearts with her movies. She describes one occasion when "a nine-year-old came up to me and said that she had been waiting her whole life to meet me. It is great to know that [films] that I have done have had such an effect on kids."[38]

She was aware of her position as a role model to young women, as well as the responsibility that goes along with it. "I don't mind being seen as a role model. But it's not something that I have ever aspired to be," she noted. Yet she did not believe that being a role model meant she had to be careful about the choices she made in her life just so that others would still approve of her. She said that her idea of a role model was "somebody that does things because of what they believe in regardless of what other people think."[39]

Off to College

At the same time that Hathaway was making princess movies, she was also busy attending college. Always a good student with a keen intelligence, she was very studious and earned good grades. By her own admission, however, her behavior in college was not always as squeaky clean as the image the public and the media had of her.

Hathaway attended Vassar College, a prestigious liberal arts college in New York. She had delayed her first semester, however, for the filming of the first *Princess Diaries* movie in the fall of 2000. When she began college in the spring of 2001, she decided to major in English with a minor in women's studies. She read great literature such as *Beowulf*, as well as works by Geoffrey Chaucer, William Shakespeare, Jane Austen, and many others. She also enjoyed her classes in philosophy, political science, American literature, and British literature.

Although Hathaway attended college on and off beginning in 2001, she found it difficult and frustrating to juggle her studies with her acting career.

Although she liked college and enjoyed making movies, she was finding it difficult to do both at the same time. She was already a semester behind in freshman English when she first started, which was frustrating for her. Equally frustrating, when she would return to classes after filming a movie, she would feel left out of conversations when her friends would discuss something from a class she had missed. She also began to feel as if she did not know herself very well or have a keen grasp of what her priorities were, and she worried that this lack of self-knowledge might lead her astray. In 2003, therefore, she decided to take a year off from acting in order to focus on college.

Hathaway had a lot of fun living the life of a typical college student. She lived in the dorms for a while, where she would hang out with her friends, eat too much, sometimes blow off writing a paper in favor of watching movies on TV, and often stay up all night. The dorm she lived in was coed, meaning that both males and females lived in the same building. "You've never lived until you've shared a dorm bathroom with 10 guys," she says. "And then walked down the hallway with zit cream all over your face."[40]

She confesses that she began smoking cigarettes and also experimented with drinking while she was in college, and she sometimes drank too much and wound up dancing atop a table. This behavior was certainly at odds with her princess-like public image. Yet because it was still relatively early in her career (the first *Princess Diaries* movie was not released until the beginning of her second semester), she was able to remain somewhat anonymous while in college and keep her behavior out of the public eye. Also, although Hathaway sometimes drank to excess at Vassar, she soon outgrew such wild behavior. "I got my partying out of my system in college,"[41] she insists.

Feeling Lost

Hathaway attended Vassar for three semesters before transferring to New York University's Tisch School of the Arts in 2005 for one semester. Since then, her many acting commitments have prevented her from completing a degree, although she would like to earn one from New York University someday.

There was a brief time while she was in college that she contemplated giving up acting altogether. In a 2003 interview she stressed that because she was in college, any movie offer would have to be very special in order for her to accept it and leave school. In part, she was tired of playing princesses. She explains that there is "only so long that you can play those as a young lady before you start feeling really ridiculous." After playing a princess in three movies, she was "ready to hang up the tiara, and put the ball-gown in storage."[42] She admits she had a lot of fun making the movies and has no regrets about them, but she did not want to get stuck playing the same kind of family-friendly roles for the rest of her career. "That's not why I became an actor," she said in 2004. "And that's not where I intend to stay."[43]

Hathaway also continued to have doubts about her own talent, and she did not think of herself as a real actress at this point in her life. "I just didn't think I was any good, and felt lost,"[44] she says. She had just about decided to give up on acting altogether when two movies came along that would change everything for her.

Chapter 3

The Princess Grows Up

After appearing in seven family-friendly movies by the time she was twenty-two, Anne Hathaway was ready to break away from her image as a role model for kids and take on edgier, adult roles. Thanks largely to her innate creativity and skill, she made a successful transition from being a teen idol to appearing in adult-themed movies when she was in her early twenties. Even while she appeared in these dramatic movies, she also took on roles in various comedies, which allowed her to show off her comedic chops. She sometimes plays offbeat characters, one of which earned her a nomination for an Academy Award.

The "Anti-Princess"

In 2005, having made her name in family-friendly films, Hathaway turned toward more gritty fare with the first two of her adult-themed movies. In the independent film *Havoc*, she plays a rich Los Angeles teenager who forms a gang with her friends and gets involved in drugs and prostitution. Although she describes the film as her "very anti-princess role,"[45] she insists that she did not accept the role merely to break away from her squeaky-clean image but rather because she was interested in the character of Allison Lang and wanted the challenge of playing her.

Hathaway's *Princess Diaries* costar Mandy Moore was originally slated to play the lead, but Hathaway took over the role when

Hathaway took the part of a troubled teenager in the 2005 film Havoc *in an effort to expand her acting experience beyond family-friendly roles.*

Moore dropped out. Moore explained that she was uncomfortable with the themes in the movie, calling *Havoc* "a film that I didn't feel ultra-comfy being a part of. It was very sexually themed and full of drugs and violence."[46] Indeed, although the eighty-five-minute movie is unrated, it contains a scene in which Hathaway is topless. It also includes several violent scenes, which Hathaway found difficult to do. "It was not fun," she confesses. "I'm not a violent person by nature and playing one was very different."[47]

The movie did not have a theatrical release in the United States, and instead went straight to video. Most critics found the film to be unoriginal and unrealistic, and several were surprised by Hathaway's leap from playing a Goody Two-shoes only the year before to appearing partially nude in this film. Her performance in the movie was generally praised, however, with one reviewer writing, "She proves without a doubt that she's been underutilized as an actress for far too long. She wholly owns the picture."[48]

A Fearless Performer

Anne Hathaway has appeared nude or partially nude in several films, including *Havoc, Brokeback Mountain*, and *Love and Other Drugs*. Her willingness to do so has earned her a reputation in Hollywood as a fearless performer, but it has also raised some eyebrows among her fans, some of whom still associate her with her many roles playing sweet, innocent young girls.

Hathaway defends her choice to appear nude in films, saying that she finds it acceptable if it is necessary to the story. "I don't actively search for [films] that I can get naked in," she says. "Nor is it something that I would ever not do a job because of."[1] She does have her limits, however; she was originally cast in the 2007 romantic comedy *Knocked Up* but dropped out over plans to use graphic footage of a woman giving birth, which she did not feel was necessary to the story. On the other hand, her film *Love and Other Drugs* was criticized by some viewers and film critics as containing excessive nudity. Hathaway admits that there is a lot of nudity in the film but thinks "none of it feels out of place. None of it feels forced. None of it feels gratuitous."[2]

1. Quoted in Kelly Marages. "Anne Hathaway Interview." *Marie Claire*, July 4, 2008. www.marieclaire.co.uk/celebrity/interviews/265792/anne-hathaway-interview.html.
2. Quoted in *Improper*. "Anne Hathaway: Nudity in *Love & Other Drugs* Shocking." November 27, 2010. www.theimproper.com/15758/anne-hathaway-nudity-in-love-other-drugs-shocking-watch.

Breaking Taboos

Although *Havoc* did not have a very wide viewership, Hathaway's next project turned out to be a blockbuster. She had a supporting role in the controversial 2005 film *Brokeback Mountain*, costarring Jake Gyllenhaal and Heath Ledger. She played Lureen Newsome, a woman whose husband carried on a lifelong secret love affair with another man.

Hathaway received great critical praise for her supporting role in the controversial film Brokeback Mountain *in 2005.*

This film got Hathaway noticed as a grown-up actress rather than a teen icon. The movie was a commercial success and also highly praised. It was nominated for numerous awards and won several, including three Academy Awards. Hathaway received critical praise for her performance in the film. One reviewer called her "compelling" and said she had a "career-best turn"[49] in the movie.

Brokeback Mountain shattered a Hollywood taboo by showing two men kissing on-screen, and Hathaway was pleased by the controversy over the film's subject matter. She embraced the fact that the movie's overt homosexual theme made many viewers uncomfortable. "I was proud of the fact that it forced people to talk about and confront their feelings,"[50] she says. In part because her older brother, Michael, is gay, this movie remains one of her favorite projects. "I'm more proud of the film than anything I have ever created."[51]

The Devil Wears Prada

Although Hathaway had only a minor role in *Brokeback Mountain*, it was enough to get her noticed as a serious dramatic actress. Movie offers began to pour in. One such offer was for the comedy-drama *The Devil Wears Prada* (2006), the screen adaptation of the best-selling Lauren Weisberger novel. Hathaway was actually approached about the project before the script was finalized—a situation that almost wound up costing her the lead. She explains, "I was their first choice, and I said, 'I'm just gonna hang back, and please come to me when you're done with the script.' So they finished the script, and Meryl Streep got on board, and suddenly it was, 'Is Reese Witherspoon available?' I went from being first choice, deal in hand, to having to wait for seven girls to turn down the part before it came to me. I was sick with worry."[52]

Another hurdle Hathaway faced was her first meeting with Streep, who has always been one of her idols. Hathaway has

Hathaway played opposite legendary actress Meryl Streep, left, in the 2006 comedy-drama The Devil Wears Prada.

often felt starstruck when meeting her famous costars, who have included Julie Andrews in *The Princess Diaries*, Cary Elwes in *Ella Enchanted*, and Heath Ledger in *Brokeback Mountain*. She was very nervous about meeting and working with the legendary Streep, who is often referred to as the best actress in American history. But Streep put Hathaway at ease during their initial meeting by hugging her and saying, "I think you're perfect for the role and I'm so happy we're going to be working on this together."[53] Working with Streep on the set of Prada "was heaven," said Hathaway. "She, as a person, is kind of who I want to be. And as an actress, she's beyond my wildest dreams."[54]

In *Prada* Hathaway plays a journalist who lands a job as an assistant to Streep's character, the tough-as-nails editor of a leading fashion magazine. Hathaway and her costar Emily Blunt had to lose weight for the film, which revolves around the fashion industry, in which everyone is stick-thin. They followed a strict diet of nothing but fruit, vegetables, and fish. Hathaway says that she and Blunt got so hungry during their grueling diet that they would "clutch at each other and cry."[55]

Critical response to *Prada* was generally favorable, with Streep, Blunt, and Hathaway all highly praised for their performances. A writer for *Elle* magazine said Hathaway turned in a performance that was "deft and graceful."[56] And a writer for the *New Yorker* praised her subtle performance, saying that "she suggests, with no more than a panicky sidelong glance, what Weisberger takes pages to describe."[57] Thanks largely to her leading role in this widely popular film, Hathaway was now considered an A-list star, and there were bigger things coming her way.

"The World's Worst Haircut"

Perhaps the movie that got Hathaway the most notice was the emotionally intense *Rachel Getting Married*. In this movie she played Kym, a model whose drug use led to tragic consequences and eventually landed her in rehab. Kym's sister, Rachel, is the one getting married, but it is Kym who demands attention with her

Hathaway's convincing performance as a troubled and flawed Kym in Rachel Getting Married *earned her the praise of the film's director, Jonathan Demme, as well as critics, and it garnered her nominations for both an Academy Award and a Golden Globe.*

behavior, which includes a rambling toast at her sister's rehearsal dinner in which she goes on at length about herself and her problems.

Hathaway was drawn in by the film the first time she read the script, which she could not put down. She recalls, "'I was in my old apartment in the West Village [in Manhattan], just pacing back and forth between the kitchen table and the couch. I somehow wound up on the floor sobbing by the last page."[58] She says that she wanted the part in *Rachel* because she wondered, "What would it be like to have a manipulative streak a mile wide that you're completely not aware of?"[59]

Hathaway worked hard to prepare for the role. For example, she had her lines memorized a year before the movie was made. Jonathan Demme, who directed *Rachel Getting Married*, was impressed by her dedication and called Hathaway a "genius" and "a great American actress."[60] Demme, who came to think of Hathaway like a daughter, predicted great things for her. "She's got a very special gift," he said. "If she chooses well, her body of work will soon be being measured alongside the greatest of the greats."[61]

Hathaway described the time she spent working on the film as "an entirely satisfying experience" and said that it helped her grow both professionally and personally. While working on *Rachel*, she realized that in her earlier films, she had tried to minimize her characters' unlikable traits in favor of their more likable ones. "That's just so . . . boring!" she says. But with her character in *Rachel*, she learned that it was okay to portray someone as flawed—and this was liberating to her because it allowed her to accept her own flaws as a human being. "It became a breakthrough in terms of my life," she says. "It was a big thing!"[62]

For her performance as Kym, who sports a sawed-off pixie that one writer referred to as "the world's worst haircut,"[63] Hathaway received high praise. The *Los Angeles Times Magazine* called her performance "ferocious."[64] *Elle* magazine praised her ability to evoke emotions that were "a tour of human complexity, at once comic, awful, raw, and wrenching."[65] And the *New York Times* pointed to "her rambling four-minute toast," which it described as "by turns bizarrely perky, hostile and self-pitying,"[66] as being especially memorable.

Getting Stitches on *Get Smart*

In real life, Anne Hathaway is every bit as clumsy as some of the characters she plays. For example, she had to use her old, bulkier BlackBerry for a while after she spilled sunscreen on her new one. "She has a bad record with phones," says her brother Michael. "She loses them pretty frequently."

This clumsy streak of hers sometimes translates into accidents on the set. For example, filming of *Get Smart* had to be halted for a day after Hathaway, who played Agent 99, was injured during a fight scene. For the scene, she was supposed to grab hold of a metal bar, lift her legs up to her chest, and kick another actor in the chest. Instead, when she lifted her legs up she accidentally struck them on another metal bar and split her shins open, revealing the bone. At first, she tried to convince the director she could finish the scene, but the director insisted she get medical attention. Hathaway wound up getting fifteen stitches to sew up the gashes in her legs.

Quoted in Ramin Setoodeh. "The Rehabilitation of Anne Hathaway." Daily Beast. *Culture* (blog), September 19, 2008. www.thedailybeast.com/newsweek/2008/09/19/the-rehabilitation-of-anne-hathaway.html.

Hathaway was nominated for an Academy Award and a Golden Globe, both for best actress. Even with all the critical acclaim she was receiving, she nevertheless remained humble about her performance, saying, "I just gave the most truthful, dynamic performance that I could think of. I just concerned myself with telling the truth."[67]

She was up against stiff competition for the Academy Award; other nominees for Best Actress included Meryl Streep and Kate Winslet, another of Hathaway's idols. She lost to Winslet, who took home the Oscar for her performance in *The Reader* (2008). Yet just being nominated for the most coveted of all acting awards is a boost to any career, and Hathaway found herself in the enviable position of being able to pick and choose from an avalanche of movie offers.

Switching It Up

Hathaway went from the heavy, serious drama of *Rachel* to the lighthearted romantic comedy *Bride Wars*, which offered her a nice change of pace. In this film, Hathaway and costar Kate Hudson play two friends who wind up having to vie for the same venue after their weddings accidentally get booked for the same day. The movie gave both Hathaway and Hudson the chance to play opposite a female peer in a comedy, something that is not very common in movies; there are plenty of male buddy-comedies, but many fewer such for women. "One thing

Hathaway starred with Kate Hudson, right, in the 2009 romantic comedy Bride Wars. *During the making of the movie, the costars became close friends.*

we were drawn to is it's a story about friendship," Hathaway says. "To actually have the story line between two women was just . . . so refreshing."[68]

Hathaway and Hudson became good friends while working on the film. Hathaway explains that the two of them hit it off right away, in part, because of "something Kate Hudson and I have in common—that level of focus and nerdiness."[69] For her part, Hudson found the experience of working with someone as devoted to moviemaking as Hathaway to be enjoyable. But it could also be a bit disconcerting: She explains that Hathaway gets into character by talking about details in the character's life that she herself has made up. Hudson says Hathaway would suddenly start talking about made-up events in her character's past, referring to "some weird place that her character has been to, which is not in the script, which is not in the movie."[70]

Although *Bride Wars* was panned by film reviewers, it was a box office success, raking in over $115 million worldwide. Hathaway was also acknowledged for her performance in the film when she won a Teen Choice Award, Choice Movie: Comedy Actress.

Anne in Wonderland

In 2010 Hathaway appeared in three films that also did very well at the box office. She was part of the ensemble cast in the romantic comedy *Valentine's Day*, which also featured Jessica Alba, Ashton Kutcher, Julia Roberts, and many other stars. For her performance Hathaway was nominated for a Teen Choice Award for top scene stealer by a female in a movie.

She appeared in yet another romantic comedy in 2010, *Love and Other Drugs*, which reunited her with her *Brokeback Mountain* costar Jake Gyllenhaal. To prepare for her role as a woman who is diagnosed with Parkinson's disease, Hathaway arranged visits to Parkinson's support groups with the assistance of the American Parkinson Disease Association. The movie progresses from a comedy in the beginning to a more serious tone, due to Hathaway's character's medical issues and physical demise. Hathaway admits

Hathaway played the White Queen in director Tim Burton's **Alice in Wonderland,** *which she has called her favorite fairy tale, in 2010.*

that although working with Gyllenhaal again was a lot of fun, the film was emotionally difficult for her to make: "I was a wreck from start to finish. . . . I cried every single day."[71]

Love and Other Drugs did well at the box office, grossing more than $2 million on its opening day. Although the movie itself received mixed reviews, its two leads were praised. Roger Ebert said Hathaway turned in "a warm, lovable performance,"[72] while London's *Daily Mail* said Hathaway "held her own opposite Gyllenhaal"[73] in the film. Hathaway and Gyllenhaal were both nominated for a Golden Globe for the movie, and she won a Satellite Award for Best Actress in a Motion Picture, Comedy or Musical.

Another film project in 2010 gave Hathaway the opportunity to work with a director she had admired for several years, Tim Burton. She was cast as the White Queen in *Alice in Wonderland*, Burton's computer animated/live action adaptation of the Lewis Carroll classic story. This project was doubly exciting for Hathaway because, as she explains, "My favorite fairy tale is 'Alice in Wonderland.'"[74]

Anne's British Accent

Anne Hathaway has adopted a British accent in several films, including *Becoming Jane, Alice in Wonderland,* and *One Day.* Her portrayals of British characters have not always been met by praise, however. In *One Day,* which was adapted from a 2009 novel by David Nicholls, Hathaway plays Emma Morley, a British woman, over the course of twenty years in Morley's life. Says Hathaway, "I don't think too many people were thrilled that an American was playing her."[1]

Critics were not very impressed by the film, and Hathaway's accent in particular was singled out for sharp criticism. A movie reviewer for *Rolling Stone* magazine said it was "bad" and "heading for infamy."[2] Indeed, *Time* magazine put her performance in *One Day* on its list of the Top 10 Worst Fake British Accents.

1. Quoted in Chelsea Handler. "Anne Hathaway." *Interview,* August 20, 2011. www .interviewmagazine.com/film/anne-hathaway-1/#_.
2. Peter Travers. "*One Day.*" *Rolling Stone,* August 18, 2011. www.rollingstone.com/ movies/reviews/one-day-20110818.

The movie, which also starred Johnny Depp as the Mad Hatter, turned out to be a huge commercial and critical success. Hathaway was once again nominated for a Teen Choice Award for scene stealer for her performance in this blockbuster.

Hathaway had become a huge star who was sought after, admired, and respected by everyone from her fans to fellow actors to producers and directors. Studios knew that putting Hathaway in a movie was likely to make the movie a financial success. In 2010 *Forbes* magazine ranked her at number two (behind Shia LaBeouf) on its list of actors who earn studios the most for their money. According to *Forbes,* for every $1 Hathaway earned in 2010, her studios made $64. Most of this came from *Alice in Wonderland,* as well as *Bride Wars,* which cost $30 million to make and earned $115 million at the global box office. Eloise Parker, the features editor for *OK!* magazine, notes: "The thing about Anne Hathaway is she's very versatile. She's not just looking for big-budget projects that offer a big-budget salary, she goes for roles that are a little more quirky, a little more interesting. *Alice in Wonderland* is a great example of that. As the White Queen, she was almost unrecognizable, and it was kind of a gamble, but it certainly paid off for her and for the studio."[75]

Still Humble

All of this success has not gone to Hathaway's head. She remains humble about her own talents and is quick to credit others for the success of her various projects. She counts herself lucky to have been given the opportunity to work with so many big-name stars and directors and is still a bit awestruck by them. "More so than a kid in a candy store," she gushes. "It's *amazing* to work with people at the top."[76]

Chapter 4

The Other Side
of Anne

Anne Hathaway's numerous films have kept her very busy. But there is another side to her professional life that keeps her just as busy. Her charitable endeavors, product endorsements, and stage and voice work help define who she is as an entertainer as well as a person.

Commercial Success

Hathaway began her professional career by appearing in commercials, and after she became a well-known actress, several companies were eager for her to endorse their products. She became a spokesperson for several, appearing in commercials and print ads.

Hathaway signed on to do advertising for the Lux Basic line of hair and skin products in 2005. She joined other well-known actresses such as Natalie Portman, Jennifer Lopez, and Catherine Zeta-Jones, who have also done promotions for Lux. She is shown swinging her famously luxurious brunette locks in the shampoo commercials and print ads, which were released in Japan only.

In 2008 Hathaway became the face of Lancôme fragrance Magnifique. The company chose the twenty-five-year-old actress in part because of her young fan base, in order to expand sales to a younger market. To launch the new perfume, Hathaway

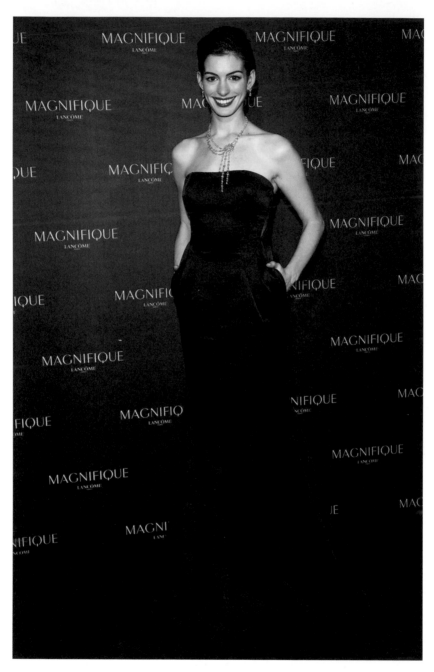

Hathaway attends a launch event in Paris, France, for the Lancôme fragrance Magnifique in 2008. She served as the perfume's spokesperson.

appeared in a floor-length black evening gown at a press conference that summer with the beauty company at the Grand Palais in Paris. The ad campaign included sophisticated TV commercials featuring her in evening wear and, in one, dancing seductively on a tabletop.

In 2011 and 2012, Hathaway appeared in print ads for Tod's Group, an Italian company that produces leather goods. The print ads, which were photographed in London, appeared in fashion magazines such as *Vogue*. In the ads, she poses with shoes and handbags for the company's Signature Collection spring campaign. Like Lancôme, Tod's wanted Hathaway because the company is aiming to attract a younger clientele. Hathaway said she was "very excited" to be part of the advertising campaign, calling herself "a longtime fan" of the company's products. "The designs are classic,"[77] she notes.

Master of Ceremonies

Another way in which Hathaway serves as a spokesperson is through hosting events. For example, in the summer of 2011 she was the master of ceremonies at the White Fairy Tale Love Ball during couture week in Paris. The event, which benefited the Naked Heart Foundation, was held at the estate of world-famous fashion designer Valentino. Hathaway wore a vintage white Valentino dress whose whimsical flounces were edged with tiny silver beads. In her hair was a tiara of acrylic flowers and gold charms that included a butterfly, clock face, and tiny fork. "Isn't that cute? It's very whimsical," Hathaway said of the tiara. She added, "I feel like a rock-star, elfin princess."[78]

Also in 2011, Hathaway was chosen, along with James Franco, to cohost the Eighty-Third Academy Awards ceremony. She had already shown she was capable of entertaining an audience at the Oscars; at the awards show in 2009, she had performed a song-and-dance routine with host Hugh Jackman, who had lifted her out of her seat in the audience and carried her onstage for the performance. As cohost in 2011, Hathaway again had a song-and-dance routine during which, in a nod

Hathaway belts out a production number during the 2011 Academy Awards telecast, which she cohosted with James Franco.

In Defense of Liu Xiaobo

In 2010, Liu Xiaobo, a Chinese writer and professor, was awarded the Nobel Peace Prize in recognition of his efforts on behalf of human rights in China. Liu was arrested in 2008 by Chinese authorities on charges of inciting subversion and sentenced to eleven years in prison. The Chinese government would not allow him or his family to attend the Nobel ceremony; instead, he was represented by an empty chair onstage while Norwegian actress Liv Ullmann read aloud an essay Liu had written for his trial. At a press conference the day after the Nobel ceremony, Anne Hathaway said:

> I was, first of all, struck by the tragedy of Liu Xiaobo's absence. Every moment had extra poignance because he wasn't there to hear it, and he was the reason that we were all there. I kept thinking about his wife, and I kept thinking about what it is to be a human being and how, when we're our best selves, we're not alone. We can't help but love each other. We can't help but reach out to each other and lean on each other. And he's done just that with his life. And with his imprisonment, he's not the only one affected. He's a son. He is a husband. He is a friend. And all those people in his life are affected, and when I heard his words, his extraordinary, poetic, beautiful words . . . I became overwhelmed with the tragedy of his situation and how very unfair it is, not just for him, but all the people he loves and all the people who matter to him.

Anne Hathaway. Speech given at press conference for the 2010 Nobel Peace Prize Concert. Oslo, Norway, December 11, 2010.

to their duet two years earlier, she serenaded Jackman in the front row, inviting him to join her on the stage. She was also well outfitted during the show, going through no fewer than eight different costume changes, including seven gowns and one tuxedo. Although many people thought Hathaway and Franco were mismatched as cohosts and that the show itself was boring, Hathaway said cohosting the Oscars made her "feel like the luckiest girl in the whole wide world. . . . I couldn't be more grateful."[79]

On a more serious note, Hathaway also cohosted the 2010 Nobel Peace Prize Concert in Oslo, Norway, with actor Denzel Washington. This concert is held every year on December 11 as a tribute to that year's Nobel Peace Prize Laureate. It features musical artists from around the world performing a variety of music, from pop and rock to jazz and classical. Performers at the 2010 concert included Barry Manilow, Elvis Costello, Herbie Hancock, and many others. The 2010 Nobel Peace Prize was awarded to imprisoned Chinese human rights activist Liu Xiaobo.

Hathaway Lends Her Voice

In addition to her many activities as a spokesperson and host, Hathaway has also lent her voice to projects in another way: as a voice artist. In 2002 she narrated the audiobook version of *The Princess Diaries* by Meg Cabot and went on to narrate the second and third installments of the series as well.

More recently, Hathaway was chosen along with Kate Winslet and Samuel L. Jackson to narrate a line of audiobooks from Audible Books. In 2012 she narrated the audiobook version of the children's classic *The Wonderful Wizard of Oz* by L. Frank Baum. Hathaway, who is a longtime fan of the 1939 film version, had never read the book before taking on this project. She loved reading the book aloud for her recording and imagined that she was reading it to her young cousins.

Hathaway has also lent her voice to several animated film and TV projects. The first of these was voicing the character of Haru in the English version of the 2002 Japanese animated film *The Cat Returns*. In this G-rated movie, which a reviewer for *Variety* described as "catchy entertainment for kids and adults,"[80] Hathaway's character is a shy, awkward teen who becomes

Hathaway attends the Hollywood premiere of Rio in 2010. She voiced a female macaw named Jewel in the animated film.

entangled with a group of felines, one of whom she rescues from the path of an oncoming truck.

In 2005 Hathaway voice was heard in another family-friendly animated film, *Hoodwinked!* In this retelling of the classic fairy tale "Little Red Riding Hood," Hathaway voices Red Puckett, who escapes from the wolf after spraying him with a can of Wolf Away. The movie got lukewarm reviews, with many complaining about the poor quality of the animation. The *Christian Science Monitor* called it a "moderately enjoyable escapade" but added that the movie was not "quite clever enough for adults and not quite imaginative enough for children."[81] A review for the Kidzworld website, however, did tout it as featuring "spunky characters, a lot of humor and plenty of kick-butt action!"[82]

In the animated film *Rio* (2011), Hathaway voiced Jewel, a female macaw. The film was a commercial and critical success, and Hathaway was nominated for a Teen Choice Award and a People's Choice Award for her performance.

Hathaway has also done voice work as a guest star on TV. She appeared in two episodes of the Fox animated sitcom *Family Guy* in 2010. That same year, she also voiced the character Princess Penelope in "Once Upon a Time in Springfield," an episode of the long-running animated Fox sitcom *The Simpsons*. Hathaway has been a fan of this show ever since she first watched it with her brothers when she was a little girl, so she was extremely excited to be invited to perform on it. This was her second guest appearance on the animated show, and she was awarded TV's highest honor, an Emmy Award, for her voice-over performance as Penelope.

Along with her voice work for audiobooks, movies, and TV, Hathaway has also done a good amount of singing in her career. A soprano who can belt out a tune with gusto, Hathaway studied singing as a teen. It is something that she loves doing, but she has never considered breaking out into a professional singing career. Nevertheless, she often sings in her films, and she is heard on the soundtracks of *Rio*, *Ella Enchanted*, and *Hoodwinked!* In the words of Tommy O'Haver, the director of *Ella Enchanted*, she is "a fantastic singer."[83]

Anne Takes the Stage

Despite all her success in films that span many different genres, Hathaway says she has never really felt comfortable acting in movies. "It's not what I trained to do," she explains. "I trained to be a theater actress."[84] In 2002 she got the chance to return to the stage she had so adored as a schoolgirl. This time, she appeared in the City Center Encores! production of *Carnival!* In her first professional stage role in New York City, she played an innocent sixteen-year-old girl named Lili during the musical's five-night run.

Hathaway was very nervous about her New York stage debut and rehearsed for two weeks with a vocal coach before the formal rehearsals began with the rest of the cast, by which time she had memorized all her songs as well as most of her lines. Her dedication and love of the stage helped earn her critical praise for her performance. Ben Brantley, a reviewer for the *New York Times*, commented that her "pretty, open face . . . looks as if it had never raised an eyebrow" and that "she trades on her novice status to create a sense of unblinking wonder." He added, "Give thanks this morning for Anne Hathaway."[85]

Hathaway found herself onstage in New York once again when she appeared in *Twelfth Night*, the Shakespeare in the Park offering for the summer of 2009. She played Viola, a shipwrecked young woman who disguises herself by wearing men's clothing. Hathaway loved everything about the experience, including the long rehearsals, getting to sing onstage, and hanging out in New York with the cast and crew. She even enjoyed getting to cross-dress for her part, and she decided to try walking around the city dressed as a boy just to help her get in character; however, as soon as she stepped outside, she was met by photographers who snapped pictures of her and posted them on the Internet. Hathaway was embarrassed to be caught in such an unflattering outfit, something she was doing to prepare for her role. All in all, though, she was exhilarated by her experiences performing Shakespeare onstage in Central Park. "It was terrifying and exhausting and thrilling—a great way to spend summer vacation,"[86] she says.

Hathaway takes a curtain call with her costars after appearing as Viola in a Shakespeare in the Park production of Twelfth Night *in New York City in 2009.*

Visiting a Giraffe Sanctuary in Africa

In 2011 Anne Hathaway traveled to Africa as part of her work with the Girl Effect charity. While in Ethiopia, she took some time to visit a giraffe sanctuary before heading off to meet with young representatives from the Berhane Hewan program. At the sanctuary, Hathaway was impressed by how beautiful the giraffes were, as well as by their long, black tongues. She describes what happened when she fed a baby giraffe named Martha at the sanctuary:

> She was really cute because she had a nice little way about her—she would just kind of gently take the food out of your hand. And then her mother came over—it was a big mamma—whose tongue was, I can't even [say how long it was]. So I was like, "Oh, do you want some food?" She took her tongue, wrapped it around my wrist in a death grip, and shoved my hand up into her mouth and *sucked*, and then let go.

Quoted in *The Ellen DeGeneres Show*. NBC, April 13, 2011.

Hathaway Steps Up

Hathaway is dedicated to her acting career, and she is equally dedicated to several causes that are close to her heart. She has provided financial support to numerous charities, including the Clinton Foundation, Oxfam, Feeding America, the Step Up Women's Network, and many others. She also contributed to *The Hollywood Cookbook*, a charitable book project that features the culinary creations of twenty celebrities and six world-class chefs, each of whom provided a favorite recipe as well as discussed their

Hathaway plays with a baby during a visit to Nicaragua in 2006 as part of a program to administer hepatitis A vaccines to children.

favorite charity. Hathaway chose to discuss the Lollipop Theater Network. She serves as a patron of and an adviser to the charity, which helps bring movies to children who are in the hospital and unable to go to a movie theater due to chronic or serious illnesses. Hathaway's efforts on behalf of children also include contributing to the St. Jude Children's Research Hospital, which also helps seriously ill children.

Hathaway has also traveled internationally as part of her philanthropic endeavors. In January 2005 she took part in the documentary *A Place in Time*, directed by her good friend actress Angelina Jolie. For the project, numerous celebrities traveled with film crews to twenty-seven locations around the world. Then, each turned on video cameras at the same time

Anne Lends a Hand

On September 11, 2001 (9/11), terrorists attacked New York City and Washington, D.C., killing nearly three thousand people. In their aftermath, many Americans were inspired to step up and do what they could to help, including residents of Millburn, New Jersey, where Anne Hathaway grew up. After 9/11, the students of Mickey McNany, the theater school director at Millburn's Paper Mill Playhouse, organized a performance to benefit the families and children of the victims. McNany contacted Hathaway and her family to ask if they were interested in helping out. Hathaway, who was in California at the time wrapping up filming of *The Princess Diaries*, told McNany she would love to lend a hand. She flew back to New Jersey to appear in the benefit. McNany recalls, "She sang and absolutely overwhelmed everyone with a beautiful song called 'We Can Be Kind.' There was not a dry eye in the house."

Quoted in Robert Levin. "Anne Hathaway: She's Still Annie from Millburn." NJ.com, February 22, 2011. www.nj.com/insidejersey/index.ssf/2011/02/shes_still_annie_from_millburn.html.

in order to capture the daily life of people around the globe at the same moment. Hathaway, who traveled to Cambodia for the documentary, was deeply moved by the experience. She said Jolie had given her "an extraordinary gift"[87] by inviting her to be part of the project.

Inspired by Jolie's numerous examples of humanitarian work around the world, Hathaway traveled to Nicaragua in 2006, where she spent a week helping vaccinate children against hepatitis A. She did not actually administer the shots because, as she put it, "that would make the kids cry even more."[88] Instead, she was in charge of applying bandages decorated with Batman, Barbie, and Dora the Explorer. Nicaraguan children have some of the highest death rates from communicable diseases in Latin America, and

Hathaway felt that she was doing truly something meaningful by helping with the vaccination program.

Hathaway's humanitarian efforts have also taken her to Africa, where she traveled as part of an initiative called the Girl Effect. This group aims to help improve conditions for impoverished adolescent girls throughout the world. As part of her work with this group, Hathaway traveled to Ethiopia in 2011 along with Maria Eitel, president of the Nike Foundation. There they met with a group of young girls from the Berhane Hewan program, which is dedicated to ending underage marriage in Africa. The girls, who ranged in age from seven to sixteen, performed a skit for Hathaway that they had written themselves about why child marriages should be stopped. After their journey, Hathaway and Eitel coauthored an article titled "What African Girls Fear More than Drought" for the news website the Daily Beast about the plight of women, especially young girls, in Africa.

Supporting Gay Rights

In addition to working to improve conditions for women and children throughout the world, there is another group whose well-being is very important to Hathaway. Ever supportive of her older brother, Michael, who is gay, Hathaway is vocal about her support for the lesbian, gay, bisexual, and transgender (LGBT) community. She is involved in various gay-rights causes, including the fight to legalize gay marriage, something that she believes every U.S. state should do. She has also given money to several organizations that protect gay rights, including the Trevor Project, which works to prevent suicides among LGBT youth, and the Human Rights Campaign, which is the largest gay civil rights organization in the nation.

In 2008 the Human Rights Campaign honored Anne Hathaway with an Ally Award. At her acceptance speech in Los Angeles, she received laughter and applause from the audience during her forthright and heartfelt speech, in which she asserted,

I believe I have received this award not so much because of what I have done, but because of the way I was born and

Hathaway attends a benefit in 2008 for the Trevor Project, one of several LGBT advocacy groups that she has publicly supported.

raised. I was born the younger sister of a gay man—my older brother, Mike—and the daughter of parents who are both empathetic to and loving of the LGBT community. . . . Just for the record, we don't feel that there is actually anything "alternative" about our family values. . . . I don't consider myself just an ally to the LGBT community; I consider myself your family. And so, I'm doing what we should all do with our families: I'm loving you, I support you, I completely accept you as you are, as I hope you do me. And if anyone, *ever*, tries to hurt you, I'm gonna give 'em hell.[89]

Chapter 5

Behind the Scenes with Anne

In her private life as well as her professional life, Anne Hathaway remains humble. She is quick to laugh at herself and downplay her accomplishments, almost as if she cannot believe how successful or famous she has become. Her friends and family remain a very important part of her life, and in 2011 she took a bold step in her romantic life.

Modest—and Funny, Too

Hathaway tends to be modest about her professional achievements. For example, she has worked with some highly regarded directors, including Ang Lee and Jonathan Demme (something she seems incredulous about). "Can you believe it?" she gushed to reporter Karen Durbin during an interview. She also tends to be jokingly self-effacing, gently putting herself down with a knowing laugh. As she said to Durbin, she would love to work with director Sofia Coppola, but, "I don't think I'm cool enough for her."[90]

In addition to her modest streak, Hathaway also has a terrific sense of humor and is frequently self-mocking. "I have the lowest of the low sense of humor. I laugh at bodily function humor, things like that," she confesses. "When something strikes me funny, it's messy, snot flying, tears everywhere. And that's just me laughing."[91]

Hathaway breaks into laughter at a press conference to promote **Love and Other Drugs** *in 2010. She is known among family, friends, and costars for her quick wit and sense of humor.*

A Pep Talk from Anne Hathaway

During a 2011 press conference for 20th Century Fox to promote the animated film *Rio*, Anne Hathaway shared her views on exercise—and life:

> Be yourself and go for it. . . . This is such a dumb example, but I don't love exercise. Some of it is more fun than others, so what I do is, if I'm on the treadmill and I don't want to finish, I look at it and say, "Okay, this is 20 minutes, versus the rest of my life. I'm going to spend the rest of my life doing so many other things, so I can do this for 20 minutes." I just think that, if you break it down into achievable goals, you'll wind up achieving more than you ever thought you could.

Quoted in Christina Radish. "Anne Hathaway, Jamie Foxx, George Lopez and Carlos Saldanha Interview *RIO*," January 31, 2011. http://collider.com/rio-interview-anne-hathaway-jamie-foxx-george-lopez/73866.

This sense of humor and lack of inhibition often manifests itself on the set. For example, while goofing around during the filming of *One Day*, Hathaway decided to moon her costar, Jim Sturgess, with unexpected results. She explains: "I decided to moon Jim one take, and I thought this would be great because he was running towards me, and the whole crew was behind me, so I thought, if I turn around none of the crew will see it and only Jim. So I did it, and I was feeling really good about myself, until I realized we were shooting on a street in Scotland and every single resident of the building that we were shooting in front of was filming us."[92]

During another incident on the set, this one while filming the latest Batman movie, *The Dark Knight Rises,* Hathaway got a little too much into character as Catwoman and accidentally smacked a stuntman in the eye with the butt of a gun. The man suffered a black eye and a splitting headache, and Hathaway was horrified by what happened. To help apologize, she bought him a silver pen that was humorously engraved with the motto, "Remember no one packs a punch like Anne."[93]

Hathaway also demonstrated her sharp wit to a TV audience one night in 2011 during a guest appearance on the TBS talk show *Conan* when she belted out a rap about the paparazzi. She explained that all the media attention surrounding her upcoming project, *The Dark Knight Rises*, got a little too intense, so she wrote a song to help herself blow off steam. Singing in the style of rapper Lil Wayne, she cupped her hands around her mouth and bellowed out, "Don't act so hotsy-totsy, [girl], I know that you from Jersey!"[94]

Forthright and Honest

In addition to being modest and funny, Hathaway is a very mature and honest person. "I've always been very independent and proactive in doing things on my own,"[95] she says. One reporter described her as "a young woman with a mind of her own, and she's not afraid to speak it."[96] Indeed, Hathaway is very forthright, and she often says whatever is on her mind without reservation, a trait she attributes to her father's influence.

Hathaway is quick to admit that she is not a submissive person. "There's quite a bit of fire in me and I do know when to step forward."[97] Part of being so unabashed about speaking her mind is the fact that she knows herself very well. "I'm a very curious person, and I like that about myself," she says. She seems to have a keen sense of her own foibles, including her tendency to interrupt others. "I just get really excited when I talk," she explains. "I jump in at the end of every sentence and nobody ever gets to finish a thought."[98]

She also has a clear vision of the kind of person she aspires to be: "I hope I'm always passionate and honest and treat people with respect," she says. "Just to be a good person, to never be afraid of things."[99]

A Close Family

A big part of making Hathaway into the person she is today is the influence of her family. She remains very close to her family and makes spending time with them a priority. She lives in New York, as does the rest of her family, and loves to get together with them

Hathaway and then boyfriend Adam Shulman, left, attend a charity ball in 2011. The couple married in September 2012.

often. She describes the experience of relaxing at home with her family as a "gorgeous blanket of nurturing familiarity."[100] Her visits with her family for the holidays consist of "pretty down-to-earth, normal stuff," she says. "I love them . . . everyone's lovely people and the food's always good."[101]

Although the entire family has moved to New York, they still enjoy visiting New Jersey, particularly scenic Cape May, which is classified as a National Historic Landmark. Hathaway estimates she has gone to Cape May with her family every summer of her whole life. One of the things she enjoys most about going there is getting to see her mother's many performances onstage, which include starring in plays such as *Steel Magnolias* and *I Hate Hamlet* at the Cape May Stage.

Hathaway continues to be close friends with both her brothers in their adulthood. She is not only outspoken in her support of her older brother's homosexuality, she is also a protective big sister. During an interview in 2008, she wondered aloud: "My little brother just left for Oxford. Does he have a comforter?" She explained, "He left two days ago and I'm freaking out. I'm really struggling with it. . . . I'm going to cry, I'm so proud of him."[102]

Hathaway's close family ties are part of the reason she lives in New York instead of in California, the seat of moviemaking. But there are other reasons she chooses to stay in the region where she grew up. "I love the seasons on the east coast,"[103] she says. She also loves attending Broadways plays and musicals, another reason she continues to live in New York.

She commutes to Los Angeles whenever necessary, staying a couple of weeks at a time. But, she says, "I can't live there. I hate cars. And I [sun]burn really easily."[104] Because of her extremely fair skin, she avoids spending time in the sun, something that is difficult to do in Los Angeles. But most of all, she is just happier and more comfortable in New York, where she feels she can truly be herself.

Hathaway's family got a little larger in September 2012, when she married longtime boyfriend and fellow actor Adam Shulman. The two were wed before 180 friends and relatives on a beautiful rustic estate in Big Sur, California, famous for its clear blue ocean vistas and stunning forest backdrops. The *Los Angeles Times* reported the actress spent about $100,000 on lush floral arrangements, and wore an elaborate, gauzy dress designed by Valentino. The couple also kept others in mind as they made their vows by donating proceeds from the sale of their wedding photos to the American Cancer Society, St. Jude Children's Research Hospital, and to non-profit organizations that fight to legalize same-sex marriage.

Annie Kicks Back

In New York, Hathaway spends a lot of time hanging out with her close friends, who call her Annie. She and her pals enjoy activities such as visiting museums and art galleries, hanging out in cafés and coffee shops, perusing bookstores, seeing movies, and having lunch together. Hathaway also loves playing Scrabble in any format, whether the board game with family and friends, an online version with other people, or just playing against her computer.

Hathaway counts British actress Emily Blunt, whom she met on the set of *Prada*, as one of her best friends. The two of them hit it off right away and have become each other's closest confidante. "It's so nice to have someone you can speak with in shorthand about directors, or annoyances, or when things are going well,"[105] Hathaway says. Another of her close friends is fellow actor Jake Gyllenhaal. The two first met when they played husband and wife in *Brokeback Mountain*, and they reunited five years later to make *Love and Other Drugs*. Gyllenhaal said in a 2010 interview that he and Hathaway share "what's starting to be a long history together, professionally and as friends."[106]

When Hathaway is not relaxing with her family or hanging out with her friends, she still enjoys unwinding alone at home. She adores dogs and has a 70-pound (32kg) chocolate Labrador named Esmeralda. She loves to curl up on the couch with a good book in her lap and Esmeralda by her side, usually while also listening to some music. Her taste in music varies; like many people, the type of music she listens to depends on the mood she is in. She loves reggae, especially Bob Marley. Other favorite performers include alternative rock band the Dandy Warhols,

Hathaway and close friend Emily Blunt celebrate the Star of the Year Awards they won for their performances in **The Devil Wears Prada** *in 2006.*

indie band the Strokes, smooth jazz band Sade, hip-hop/neo soul band the Roots, Icelandic singer-songwriter Björk, and spoken-word artist Jill Scott.

She also has a flair for interior decorating and loves to shop at antique fairs or browse through furniture stores in Manhattan.

She has developed a knack for taking a piece of furniture and refashioning or refinishing it to suit her tastes. Consequently, she is interested in studying carpentry so that she can learn how to make her own furniture someday.

Romantic Life

Hathaway has had several romantic relationships. She dated actor Topher Grace when she was in her late teens before striking up a relationship with New York restaurateur Scott Sartiano. Neither of these relationship lasted longer than a couple of months, although she remains friends with Grace and costarred with him in *Valentine's Day*. In 2003 she began dating English actor Hugh Dancy, who played Prince Charmont in *Ella Enchanted*, but this relationship also did not last very long.

Then in 2004 she began dating Italian real estate developer Raffaello Follieri. They dated for four years and even began living together in his Manhattan condo. The couple enjoyed the high life, traveling on yachts and staying in five-star hotels. Hathaway and Follieri were in love. But in 2008, things started to fall apart. When Follieri began to have money trouble, Hathaway took over paying the rent on his condo, which came to thirty-seven thousand dollars a month. Then the government began investigating the Follieri Foundation, a charitable group Follieri had set up and Hathaway had contributed to. She became uncomfortable with the situation and ended their relationship in June 2008.

Shortly after Hathaway broke things off with Follieri, he was arrested and charged with fraud for allegedly scamming more than $2 million from investors. An investigation revealed that he had lied to investors, and Hathaway, about his education, background, financial standing, and connections with the Vatican in order to solicit investors in his real estate business. Follieri then misused millions of dollars of investors' money to finance his extravagant personal expenses, including clothing, cosmetics, flowers, expensive dinners, jewelry, wine, and yacht rentals for himself, his parents, and Hathaway.

Hathaway dated Italian real estate developer Raffaello Follieri, right, for four years until he was brought up on business fraud charges in 2008.

Although she was no longer in a relationship with Follieri, Hathaway now found herself embroiled in the scandal. She was questioned by the FBI and, although cleared of any involvement in or knowledge of his fraudulent activities, the agents confiscated all the jewelry Follieri had given her, including a gold Rolex watch, two gold rings, a pair of diamond earrings, and a five-strand pearl necklace, to use as evidence. The FBI also confiscated her personal diaries from the past four years as part of their investigation into Follieri's illegal activities. Although Hathaway willingly turned over her jewelry and diaries, she must have felt her privacy had been invaded to a certain degree; she once revealed in an interview that she had been keeping diaries since the age of fourteen but had never shared them with anyone. "I would never give it to someone and say, 'Hey, here's my soul,'"[107] she said.

That fall, Follieri was found guilty of fraud and money laundering and was sentenced to four and a half years in prison. For the first time in her career, Hathaway found herself the subject of nasty rumors and tabloid stories. She was stunned by what had happened and struggled to understand how someone she had loved and had lived with could violate the trust of others so completely. "I've never had to deal with anybody lying to me," she said. "I just didn't realize people could be like that."[108]

Although it was difficult for her to talk about the incident, she was asked about it over and over during interviews and on talk shows. She would have preferred to stay home and keep the telephone unplugged until the controversy had died down, but at the time, she was under contract to promote *Rachel Getting Married* and was obligated to make various public appearances. "I hate talking about the breakup, because I don't want it to define me," she said to *Vogue* magazine. "But as is to be expected, there were a lot of lingering trust issues."[109] One year after Follieri's arrest, she was still trying to find a way to come to grips with the situation and was moved to tears when asked about it during an interview in the summer of 2009. "I don't have the words to describe that yet," she said. "All I can say is that it was heavy, it was shocking, and I don't completely understand it."[110] Hathaway is still grateful to her brother Michael, who worked as her personal assistant for several years, for being by her side throughout the ordeal.

A Bit of Light Summer Reading

A former English major, Hathaway continues to be a voracious reader; she showed up for one interview with a dog-eared copy of Indian leader Mohandas Gandhi's autobiography tucked under her arm. Much like her taste in music, she has an eclectic taste when it comes to literature. One of her favorite authors is Ayn Rand, whose works include the best-selling novels *The Fountainhead* and *Atlas Shrugged*. Hathaway has also enjoyed reading the novels *Sophie's World* by Jostein Gaarder and *Empress Orchid* by Anchee Min, as well as the essay *Self-Reliance* by Ralph Waldo Emerson.

She was deeply moved while reading *Letters to a Young Poet* by Rainer Maria Rilke, which consists of ten letters Rilke wrote to a man who was trying to decide whether to pursue a career as a writer or stay in the army. "They're so, so beautiful," Hathaway says of the letters. She also tackled the 1981 novel *Midnight's Children* by Salman Rushdie, which deals with India's struggles to become an independent nation in the mid-twentieth century. Hathaway chose the 450-page work of historical fiction, which is listed as one of the Great Books of the 20th Century by Penguin Books, for her reading material during her summer vacation in Positano, Italy, in 2011.

Quoted in Lynn Barker. "The 'Enchanting' Anne Hathaway." TeenHollywood.com, April 7, 2004. www.teenhollywood.com/2004/04/07/the-enchanting-anne-hathaway.

Finding Love Again

Hathaway had suffered a terrible blow in her personal life, but it was not long before she found love again. A few months after ending her relationship with Follieri, mutual friends introduced her to jewelry designer and actor Adam Shulman. Hathaway and Shulman clicked immediately, and they began dating in the fall of 2008. The two soon fell in love, and Hathaway (and Esmeralda)

Hathaway and Shulman walk their dog, Esmeralda, on the streets of Brooklyn in October 2012.

moved into his Brooklyn apartment with him. After dating for three years, they announced their engagement in November 2011.

In February 2012 the couple's parents hosted an engagement party for them at Housing Works Bookstore Café in New York City. At the party, which was attended by 125 people, Hathaway happily flashed her emerald-cut diamond engagement ring, which was codesigned by Shulman. As Hathaway does not eat meat, the party featured veggie burgers, cupcakes, and truffle macaroni and cheese—all vegetarian fare. According to one partygoer, "Anne had a smile on her face all night long."[111]

Hathaway once referred to love as "one of the most wonderful parts about being alive,"[112] and she certainly seems to have found her true love. She says that, in a flash of inspiration, she came to a new understanding of marriage while watching the royal wedding of Prince William and Kate Middleton in April 2011: "You marry your best friend. That's the new fairy tale."[113] She not only feels as though she is marrying her best friend, but also that Shulman is someone she can trust. As she approached her thirtieth birthday in November 2012, Hathaway had gained a maturity and a new perspective on life and love. "What is love?" she once asked. "Honestly love is knowing someone's faults and sticking around. And I'd argue there's an addendum to that. Love is letting someone else see your faults and letting them stick around."[114]

The Future for Hathaway

Hathaway has continued to stay very busy with her career, and she has several projects in the works. She plays the iconic character Catwoman in *The Dark Knight Rises*, which was released in 2012. Pictures of Hathaway in the black leather Catwoman costume helped generate a lot of buzz for the movie before its release.

Another release in 2012 was a film version of *Les Misérables*, in which she and Hugh Jackman got the chance to capitalize on their obvious chemistry together at the Oscars. In this musical, she plays the part of Fantine—the same part her mother played when Anne was a child. For this part, Hathaway again lost weight; she also showed her dedication to acting by chopping off her luxurious hair.

A Healthy Approach to Life

Anne Hathaway has a healthy approach to life. She does not drink to excess or do drugs. She did smoke cigarettes occasionally while in college, a habit she continued off and on for several years. While filming *Rachel Getting Married*, however, she began smoking heavily, because her character smoked. By late 2008, however, Hathaway had quit smoking for good.

Today Hathaway is a vegetarian, although she confesses, "I was a terrible vegetarian for fifteen years. Terrible. Eating meat and everything." In fact, a favorite food of hers was sushi. Then she read the book *Eating Animals* by Jonathan Safran Foer, which details the sometimes deplorable conditions for animals raised for human consumption. The book prompted her to give up eating meat for good, including fish.

Quoted in *The Ellen DeGeneres Show*. NBC, April 13, 2011.

Hathaway loves learning all she can about the movie industry. For example, she served as an intern on the set of *Becoming Jane* in 2007. Now she is ready to try her hand at producing a movie with the thriller *Puzzler*, in which she will also star. As busy as she is juggling projects, Hathaway still has time to daydream about other projects she would like to do or people she would like to work with someday. She would love to work with some of her favorite directors, including Guillermo del Toro, Quentin Tarantino, Gus Van Sant, Sarah Polley, Cameron Crowe, and Terry Gilliam. She would also love to work again with Jonathan Demme, who directed her in *Rachel Getting Married*. There are also several actresses she admires and would like to work with, including Tilda Swinton, Cate Blanchett, and Emma Thompson.

Hathaway would also adore playing Kate Middleton, the Duchess of Cambridge, in a biopic if the chance arose—and after all, she has experience playing a princess in three hit films. "I'm

Hathaway chopped off her hair and lost weight to play the role of Fantine in the movie adaptation of **Les Miserables** *in 2012.*

obsessed with Kate Middleton. *Obsessed*," she says. "I loved the Royal Wedding. . . . As soon as I saw her I was utterly charmed. I'm just completely enchanted by Kate and William. With everything she's doing right now, I say, 'Yay, Kate.'" She especially loves Kate's hair, which she describes as "bouncy," but adds, "All the things that must be done to allow the crown to stay on . . . I can't even imagine."[115]

Edward Zwick, who directed *Love and Other Drugs*, has high praise for Hathaway, saying that she is "at the height of her powers, her sexuality, her craft, her ambition, and many other aspects of her personal life—all of which find their way into her work."[116] Whatever Hathaway chooses to do in her life and with her career, it seems certain that her dedication to her craft will ensure she continues to be a success.

Introduction: The Real Deal

1. Quoted in *Vogue*. "*Vogue* Diaries: Anne Hathaway." Video, October 18, 2010. www.vogue.com/videos/anne-hathaway.
2. Adam Green. "Happily Ever After: Anne Hathaway." *Vogue*, October 12, 2010. www.vogue.com/magazine/article/november-cover-anne-hathaway/#1.
3. Ramin Setoodeh. "The Rehabilitation of Anne Hathaway." Daily Beast. *Culture* (blog), September 19, 2008. www.thedailybeast.com/newsweek/2008/09/19/the-rehabilitation-of-anne-hathaway.html.
4. Quoted in Green. "Happily Ever After."
5. Quoted in Naveen N. Srivatsa. "Anne Hathaway Selected for Pudding Woman of the Year." *Harvard Crimson*, January 13, 2010. www.thecrimson.com/article/2010/1/13/pudding-smolinsky-hathaway-role.
6. Quoted in David Carr. "From a Goofy Smile to a Baring of Teeth." *New York Times*, December 31, 2008. www.nytimes.com/2009/01/04/movies/awardsseason/04carr.html?pagewanted=all.
7. Quoted in Amy Larocca. "Her Enchanted Evenings." *New York*, June 21, 2009. http://nymag.com/guides/summer/2009/57459.
8. Quoted in Karen Durbin. "Anne Hathaway." *Elle*, October 17, 2008. www.elle.com/Pop-Culture/Cover-Shoots/Anne-Hathaway.
9. Quoted in Chelsea Handler. "Anne Hathaway." *Interview*, August 20, 2011. www.interviewmagazine.com/film/anne-hathaway-1/#_.

Chapter 1: The World of Pretend

10. Quoted in Paul Fischer. "Star Talk: Anne Hathaway." Cranky Critic. www.crankycritic.com/qa/pf_articles/annehathaway.html.

11. Quoted in Associated Press. "Anne Hathaway Learns from a Legend in 'Prada.'" MSNBC, June 27, 2006. http://msnbc.msn.com/id/13463798/site/todayshow/ns/today-entertainment/t/anne-hathaway-learns-legend-prada/#.T4c1GdWyH8g.

12. Quoted in *CosmoGIRL!* "Anne Hathaway on School, Studs and Singledom." April 16, 2004. www.ivillage.com/anne-hathaway-school-studs-and-singledom-0/1-a-33670.

13. Quoted in Associated Press. "Anne Hathaway Learns from a Legend in 'Prada.'"

14. Quoted in Lynn Barker. "The 'Enchanting' Anne Hathaway." Teen Hollywood, April 7, 2004. www.teenhollywood.com/2004/04/07/the-enchanting-anne-hathaway.

15. Quoted in Contactmusic.com. "Hathaway Dreamed of Being a Nun," September 12, 2006. www.contactmusic.com/news/hathaway-dreamed-of-being-a-nun_1007990.

16. Anne Hathaway. "Anne Hathaway at 2008 HRC Los Angeles Dinner." *Huffpost Gay Voices* (blog). www.huffingtonpost.com/2012/03/08/stars-gay-siblings-hollywood_n_1333829.html.

17. Quoted in Barker. "The 'Enchanting' Anne Hathaway."

18. Quoted in *Parade*. "Wedding Bells for Anne Hathaway?," January 7, 2009. www.parade.com/celebrity/celebrity-parade/archive/anne-hathaway.html.

19. Quoted in Robert Levin. "Anne Hathaway: She's Still Annie from Millburn." NJ.com, February 22, 2011. www.nj.com/insidejersey/index.ssf/2011/02/shes_still_annie_from_millburn.html.

20. Quoted in *Parade*. "Wedding Bells for Anne Hathaway?"

21. Quoted in Jesse McKinley. "An A for Aplomb Onstage, and Political Science in the Wings." NYTimes.com, February 18, 2002. www.nytimes.com/2002/02/18/theater/an-a-for-aplomb-onstage-and-political-science-in-the-wings.html.

22. Quoted in Handler. "Anne Hathaway."
23. Quoted in Gareth Pearce. "Anne Hathaway: 'Don't Take Things Too Seriously—Especially Yourself.'" Woman. *Sun*, February 28, 2012. www.thesun.co.uk/sol/homepage/woman/4155975/Anne-Hathaway-news-One-Day-actress-reveals-how-her-mum-taught-her-to-have-a-sense-of-humour.html.
24. Quoted in Rebecca Murray. "Anne Hathaway Talks About 'Princess Diaries 2: Royal Engagement.'" About.com, August 8, 2004. http://movies.about.com/library/weekly/aapd2ah080804a.htm.
25. Quoted in Green. "Happily Ever After."
26. Quoted in Carr. "From a Goofy Smile to a Baring of Teeth."
27. Quoted in Barker. "The 'Enchanting' Anne Hathaway."

Chapter 2: Hollywood Princess

28. Quoted in Murray. "Anne Hathaway Talks About 'Princess Diaries 2.'"
29. Quoted in Julie Andrews Online. "*Princess Diaries 2: A Royal Engagement* Curiosities." www.julieandrewsonline.com/princessdiaries2_curios.html.
30. Quoted in Murray. "Anne Hathaway Talks About 'Princess Diaries 2.'"
31. Ben Falk. "*The Princess Diaries* (2001)." BBC, December 11, 2001. www.bbc.co.uk/films/2001/11/29/the_princess_diaries_2001_review.shtml.
32. Green. "Happily Ever After."
33. Quoted in McKinley. "An A for Aplomb Onstage, and Political Science in the Wings."
34. Quoted in Rebecca Murray. "Anne Hathaway on 'Ella Enchanted' and Her Princess Roles." About.com, March 31, 2004. http://movies.about.com/cs/ellaenchanted/a/elenah033104_2.htm.
35. Roger Ebert. "*Ella Enchanted*." *Chicago Sun-Times*, April 9, 2004. http://rogerebert.suntimes.com/apps/pbcs.dll/article?AID=/20040409/REVIEWS/404090304/1023.

36. Quoted in Murray. "Anne Hathaway on 'Ella Enchanted' and Her Princess Roles."
37. Quoted in Murray. "Anne Hathaway on 'Ella Enchanted' and Her Princess Roles."
38. Quoted in Neils Hesse. "*Ella Enchanted.*" Phase9 Entertainment. www.phase9.tv/moviefeatures/ellaenchantedfeature.shtml.
39. Quoted in Murray. "Anne Hathaway on 'Ella Enchanted' and Her Princess Roles."
40. Quoted in McKinley. "An A for Aplomb Onstage, and Political Science in the Wings."
41. Quoted in Associated Press. "Anne Hathaway Learns from a Legend in 'Prada.'"
42. Quoted in Fischer. "Star Talk."
43. Quoted in Tim Cooper. "Anne Hathaway: The Reluctant Princess." *Independent* (London), October 15, 2004. www .independent.co.uk/arts-entertainment/films/features/anne-hathaway-the-reluctant-princess-6159989.html.
44. Quoted in Carr. "From a Goofy Smile to a Baring of Teeth."

Chapter 3: The Princess Grows Up

45. Quoted in Murray. "Anne Hathaway on 'Ella Enchanted' and Her Princess Roles."
46. Quoted in MTV.com. "For the Record: Quick News on Britney Spears, the Roots, R. Kelly and Baby, Phil Spector, Mandy Moore & More," November 3, 2003. www.mtv.com/ news/articles/1480143/.jhtml.
47. Quoted in Murray. "Anne Hathaway on 'Ella Enchanted' and Her Princess Roles."
48. Christopher Null. "*Havoc.*" Filmcritic.com, December 1, 2005. www.filmcritic.com/reviews/2005/havoc.
49. David Dylan Thomas. "*Brokeback Mountain.*" Filmcritic. com, March 10, 2009. www.filmcritic.com/reviews/2005/ brokeback-mountain.

50. Quoted in Helen Barlow. "No Plain Jane." *Courier-Mail* (Brisbane, Australia), March 31, 2007. www.courier mail.com.au/entertainment/movies/no-plain-jane/story-e6freqex-1111113246589.

51. Quoted in iVillage. "Anne Hathaway Interview." www.ivillage.co.uk/anne-hathaway-interview/80315?field_pages=0.

52. Quoted in *Los Angeles Times Magazine*. "Anne Hathaway: Face Forward." February 2009. www.latimesmagazine.com/2009/02/anne-hathaway-jenny-lumet.html.

53. Quoted in Amelia Hill. "The Secret of Success? Kindness." *Observer* (London), October 8, 2006. http://observer.guardian.co.uk/focus/story/0,,1890311,00.html.

54. Quoted in Hanh Nguyen. "'Prada' Star Hathaway Doesn't Like It Haute." *Chicago Tribune*, June 27, 2006. www.chicagotribune.com/topic/zap-annehathawaydevilwearsprada,0,2647284.story.

55. Quoted in Contactmusic.com. "Hathaway 'Starved' on *Devil Wears Prada*," June 10, 2008. www.contactmusic.com/news/hathaway-starved-on-devil-wears-prada_1070987.

56. Durbin. "Anne Hathaway."

57. David Denby. "Dressed to Kill." *New Yorker*, July 10, 2006. www.newyorker.com/archive/2006/07/10/060710crci_cinema#ixzz1sbo3mv7V.

58. Quoted in Naomi West. "Anne Hathaway: Oscar Contender Who Is the Real Deal." *Telegraph* (London), January 9, 2009. www.telegraph.co.uk/culture/film/starsandstories/4125213/Anne-Hathaway-Oscar-contender-who-is-the-real-deal.html.

59. Quoted in Carr. "From a Goofy Smile to a Baring of Teeth."

60. Quoted in Durbin. "Anne Hathaway."

61. Quoted in West. "Anne Hathaway."

62. Quoted in Chris Lee. "Anne Hathaway Gets Serious." The Envelope. *Los Angeles Times*, November 5, 2008. http://theenvelope.latimes.com/awards/emmys/la-en-hathaway5-2008nov05,0,1547668.story.

63. Durbin. "Anne Hathaway."
64. *Los Angeles Times Magazine.* "Anne Hathaway."
65. Durbin. "Anne Hathaway."
66. Stephen Holden. "Public Speaking, Train-Wreck Style." *New York Times*, December 31, 2008. www.nytimes .com/2009/01/04/movies/awardsseason/04hold.html.
67. Quoted in Brad Balfour. "Anne Hathaway Celebrates *Rachel Getting Married* and Her Oscar Nom." PopEntertainment .com, February 16, 2009. www.popentertainment.com/ annehathaway.htm.
68. Quoted in Rachel Abramowitz. "'Bride Wars' Stars Kate Hudson and Anne Hathaway Are Funny Allies." *Los Angeles Times*, January 9, 2009. http://articles.latimes.com/2009/ jan/09/entertainment/et-bride9.
69. Quoted in *Los Angeles Times Magazine.* "Anne Hathaway."
70. Quoted in Abramowitz. "'Bride Wars' Stars Kate Hudson and Anne Hathaway Are Funny Allies."
71. Quoted in Green. "Happily Ever After."
72. Roger Ebert. *"Love and Other Drugs." Chicago Sun-Times*, November 23, 2010. http://rogerebert.suntimes.com/apps/ pbcs.dll/article?AID=/20101123/REVIEWS/101129991.
73. *Mail Online.* "Raising the Bar: Oscar Hosts Anne Hathaway and James Franco Join 13 Other Hollywood Stars in Elegant *Vanity Fair* Fold-Out Cover," February 2, 2011. www .dailymail.co.uk/tvshowbiz/article-1352699/Vanity-Fair-2011-Hollywood-issue-Oscar-hosts-Anne-Hathaway-James-Franco.html#ixzz1sENXzUfy.
74. Quoted in *Women's Wear Daily.* "A White Night at the White Fairy Tale Love Ball," July 7, 2011. www.wwd.com/eye/ design/white-night-3705425.
75. Quoted in Forbes.com. "Bang for Your Buck Actors." Video. www.forbes.com/2010/08/30/best-actors-for-the-buck-business-entertainment-actors.html.
76. Quoted in *Vogue.* "*Vogue* Diaries."

Chapter 4: The Other Side of Anne

77. Quoted in *People*. "Check Out Anne Hathaway's Latest TOD's Ad," January 6, 2012. http://stylenews.people-stylewatch.com/2012/01/06/anne-hathaway-tods-spring-2012-ads.

78. Quoted in *Women's Wear Daily*. "A White Night at the White Fairy Tale Love Ball."

79. Quoted in Sarah Bull. "Hasn't Anne Read the Reviews? Hathaway Celebrates like SHE Won an Oscar." *Mail Online*, February 28, 2011. www.dailymail.co.uk/tvshowbiz/article-1361380/Oscars-2011-Hasnt-Anne-Hathaway-read-reviews-host-celebrates-like-won.html#ixzz1scKDFThX.

80. Lisa Nesselson. "The Cat Returns." *Variety*, August 29, 2003. www.variety.com/review/VE1117921661?refcatid=31.

81. Peter Rainer. "*Hoodwinked*." *Christian Science Monitor*, January 13, 2006. www.csmonitor.com/2006/0113/p14s01-almo.html.

82. Kidzworld. "*Hoodwinked* DVD Review." www.kidzworld.com/article/6343-hoodwinked-dvd-review.

83. Quoted in Murray. "Anne Hathaway on 'Ella Enchanted' and Her Princess Roles."

84. Quoted in Associated Press. "Anne Hathaway Learns from a Legend in 'Prada.'"

85. Ben Brantley. "A Girl Innocent Enough to Believe a Puppet Is Alive." *New York Times*, February 9, 2002. http://theater.nytimes.com/mem/theater/treview.html?_r=1&html_title=&tols_title=CARNIVAL%20(PLAY)&byline=By%20BEN%20BRANTLEY&pdate=20020209&id=1077011429506.

86. Quoted in Green. "Happily Ever After."

87. Quoted in iVillage. "Anne Hathaway Interview."

88. Buck Wolfe. "'Devil' Can't Keep Hathaway from Nicaraguan Kids," July 26, 2006. http://abcnews.go.com/Entertainment/story?id=2238937#.T6BpuKtST9o.

89. Hathaway. "Anne Hathaway at 2008 HRC Los Angeles Dinner."

Chapter 5: Behind the Scenes with Anne

90. Quoted in Durbin. "Anne Hathaway."
91. Quoted in *Parade*. "Anne Hathaway's Low Sense of Humor," May 28, 2008. www.parade.com/celebrity/articles/080528-anne-hathaway.
92. Quoted in *HuffPost Celebrity* (blog). "Hathaway: I Mooned Co-star on Set of 'One Day.'" Video, August 9, 2011. www.huffingtonpost.com/2011/08/09/hathaway_n_922277.html?icid=maing-grid10%7Chtmlws-main-bb%7Cdl10%7Csec3_lnk2%7C85030.
93. Quoted in *Sun* (London). "Man Hurt by Anne Hathaway's Butt," June 17, 2011. www.thesun.co.uk/sol/homepage/showbiz/bizarre/3622096/Man-hurt-by-Anne-Hathaways-butt.html#ixzz1Oald4IZ5.
94. Anne Hathaway. *Conan*. "The Dr. and Mrs. Howard P. Reynolds Foundation Murders." TBS, August 16, 2011. Available at www.youtube.com/watch?v=uKvQvWTZFWg&feature=topvideos_entertainment.
95. Quoted in Barker. "The 'Enchanting' Anne Hathaway."
96. Cooper. "Anne Hathaway."
97. Quoted in *Parade*. "Wedding Bells for Anne Hathaway?"
98. Quoted in Handler. "Anne Hathaway."
99. Quoted in Barker. "The 'Enchanting' Anne Hathaway."
100. Quoted in Larocca. "Her Enchanted Evenings."
101. Anne Hathaway. *The Daily Show with Jon Stewart*. Comedy Central, December 1, 2008. www.thedailyshow.com/watch/mon-december-1-2008/anne-hathaway.
102. Quoted in Lee. "Anne Hathaway Gets Serious."
103. Quoted in Barlow. "No Plain Jane."
104. Quoted in Cooper. "Anne Hathaway."
105. Quoted in West. "Anne Hathaway."
106. Quoted in Green. "Happily Ever After."
107. Quoted in It's My Life. "Anne Hathaway." PBS Kids. http://pbskids.org/itsmylife/celebs/interviews/anne.html.
108. Quoted in Setoodeh. "The Rehabilitation of Anne Hathaway."

109. Quoted in Green. "Happily Ever After."
110. Quoted in Larocca. "Her Enchanted Evenings."
111. Quoted in Isley Kasica and Dahvi Shira. "Anne Hathaway Has Engagement Party in N.Y.C." *People*, February 7, 2012. www.people.com/people/article/0,,20567895,00.html.
112. Quoted in Levin. "Anne Hathaway."
113. Quoted Handler. "Anne Hathaway."
114. Quoted in Setoodeh. "The Rehabilitation of Anne Hathaway."
115. Quoted in Handler. "Anne Hathaway."
116. Quoted in Green. "Happily Ever After."

1982

Anne Jacqueline Hathaway is born on November 12 in Brooklyn, New York.

1993

Begins appearing in plays at Millburn's Paper Mill Playhouse.

1997

Makes her first TV commercial, for Better Homes and Gardens Real Estate

1999

Studies acting with the Barrow Group Theater Company in Manhattan; performs as a member of the All-Eastern United States High School Honors Chorus at Carnegie Hall in New York City; gets her first big break on the short-lived Fox Network series *Get Real*.

2000

Is nominated for a for a Teen Choice Award for Best Actress in a Drama for *Get Real*; graduates from Millburn High School; postpones her first semester of college to film *The Princess Diaries*.

2001

Attends Vassar College, majoring in English and women's studies; appears in *The Princess Diaries* and *The Other Side of Heaven*; is nominated for Teen Choice Award and an MTV Movie Award for Best Breakthrough Performance for *The Princess Diaries*; named by *People* as one of the 25 Most Intriguing People of 2001; makes *Teen People's* list of the Hottest Stars Under 25.

2002

Appears in *Nicholas Nickleby*, the big-screen adaptation of the Charles Dickens classic novel; voices Haru in the English version of the Japanese animated film *The Cat Returns*; makes her New York stage debut in the City Center Encores! production of *Carnival!*

2004

Plays a princess in two more films, *Elle Enchanted* and *The Princess Diaries 2: Royal Engagement*; begins long-term relationship with Italian real estate developer Raffaello Follieri.

2005

Transfers to Tisch School of the Arts, which she attends for one semester; voices Red Puckett in the animated movie *Hoodwinked!*; appears in *Havoc* and *Brokeback Mountain*; takes part in Angelina Jolie's documentary *A Place in Time*.

2006

Costars with Emily Blunt and Meryl Streep in *The Devil Wears Prada*; travels to Nicaragua to help vaccinate children against hepatitis A.

2007

Plays Jane Austen in *Becoming Jane*.

2008

Appears in *Get Smart*, *Passengers*, and *Rachel Getting Married*; becomes the face of Lancôme fragrance Magnifique; is presented an Ally Award from the Human Rights Campaign; breaks up with Follieri shortly before he is arrested and charged with fraud; Hathaway is questioned by the FBI but cleared of any involvement in Follieri's illegal activities; Hathaway begins dating actor Adam Shulman.

2009

Is nominated for an Academy Award and a Golden Globe Award for *Rachel Getting Married*; performs a song-and-dance routine with host Hugh Jackman at the Oscars ceremony; appears in *Bride Wars* with Kate Hudson; appears onstage in New York again, in Shakespeare's *Twelfth Night*.

2010

Appears in *Valentine's Day*, *Alice in Wonderland*, and *Love and Other Drugs*; wins a Satellite Award for Best Actress for *Love and Other Drugs*; is nominated for a Teen Choice Award for Female Movie Scene Stealer for both *Valentine's Day* and *Alice in Wonderland*; receives an Emmy Award for her voice performance in an episode of the Fox sitcom *The Simpsons*; cohosts the 2010 Nobel Peace Prize Concert in Oslo, Norway, with Denzel Washington.

2011

Voices Jewel, a female macaw, in animated film *Rio* and is nominated for a Teen Choice Award and a People's Choice Award for her performance; reunites with *Brokeback Mountain* costar Jake Gyllenhaal to make *One Day*; cohosts the Eighty-Third Academy Awards ceremony with James Franco; begins appearing in print ads for Italian leather goods company Tod's Group; announces engagement to Adam Shulman.

2012

Narrates the audiobook version of *The Wonderful Wizard of Oz* by L. Frank Baum; plays Catwoman in *The Dark Knight Rises*; begins filming *Les Misérables*; marries longtime boyfriend Adam Shulman in Big Sur, California.

For More Information

Books

L. Frank Baum. *The Wonderful Wizard of Oz*. Newark, NJ: Audible Books, 2012. Anne Hathaway lends her voice to this audio version of the classic children's tale.

Meg Cabot. *The Princess Diaries*. New York: HarperTeen, 2008. In this first installment of the series, American high schooler Mia Thermopolis suddenly finds out that she is royalty.

Gail Carson Levine. *Ella Enchanted*. New York: HarperTeen, 2004. This Newberry Honor book is a clever retelling of the classic tale of Cinderella.

Lauren Weisberger. *The Devil Wears Prada*. New York: Broadway, 2004. This best-selling novel details the struggles of a young college graduate who finds herself the assistant to a demanding boss.

Periodicals

Associated Press. "First Look: 'The Dark Knight Rises' Ends Latest Batman Trilogy with More Violence." *Washington Post*, April 24, 2012.

Olivia Barker and Maria Puente. "Anne Hathaway Sees a Gem in Fiancé Adam Shulman." *USA Today*, November 28, 2011.

Michael Cieply and Brooks Barnes. "Younger Audience Still Eludes the Oscars." *New York Times*, February 28, 2011.

Elisa Doucette. "Anne Hathaway: A Good Representation of Young Women?" *Forbes*, February 28, 2011.

Christina Everett. "Anne Hathaway, Adam Shulman Engaged." *New York Daily News*, November 28, 2011.

Brent Lang. "Anne Hathaway Sings in 'Les Misérables' at CinemaCon." *Chicago Tribune*, April 27, 2012.

Internet Sources

Cosmopolitan. "*Cosmo* Chats: Anne Hathaway and Jake Gyllenhaal," May 4, 2011. www.cosmopolitan.com.au/celebrity /cosmo-celeb-chat/2011/5/cosmo-chats-anne-hathaway-and-jake-gyllenhaal.

Nicole Eggenberger. "Anne Hathaway Debuts Drastically Skinny Look on *Les Misérables* Set." *Us Weekly*, April 19, 2012. www.usmagazine.com/celebrity-news/news/anne-hathaway -debuts-drastically-skinny-look-on-les-miserables-set-2012194#ixzz1tHIPDlMk.

Anne Hathaway and Maria Eitel. "What African Girls Fear More than Drought." Daily Beast, August 23, 2011. www .thedailybeast.com/articles/2011/08/23/anne-hathaway-maria eitel-what-african-girls-fear-more-than-drought.html.

Emma Koonse. "Anne Hathaway Throws 'Fun' Engagement Party." *Christian Post*, March 28, 2012. www.christianpost.com/news/ anne-hathaway-throws-fun-engagement-party-72239.

Daniel Miller. "Anne Hathaway Set to Produce, Star in 'Puzzler' at Paramount (Exclusive)." *Hollywood Reporter*, October 26, 2011. www.hollywoodreporter.com/news/anne-hathaway-puzzler-produce-253677.

Rebecca Murray. "Inside 'Rio' with Anne Hathaway, Jamie Foxx, and George Lopez." About.com, January 28, 2011. http:// movies.about.com/od/rio/a/rio-cast-interview.htm.

Justin Ravitz. "Breaking News: Anne Hathaway Engaged to Adam Shulman!" *Us Weekly*, November 28, 2011. www.usmagazine .com/celebrity-news/news/anne-hathaway-engaged-to-adam-shulman-20112811#ixzz1tHdm5UWS.

Sandy Schaefer. "Tom Hardy & Anne Hathaway Talk 'Dark Knight Rises' Villains." Screen Rant, April 12, 2012. http://screenrant .com/dark-knight-rises-tom-hardy-anne-hathaway-interview-sandy-164473.

Mario Testino. "Anne Hathaway for *Vogue US*, November 2010 by Mario Testino." Fashion Gone Rogue, October 18, 2010. http:// fashiongonerogue.com/anne-hathaway-vogue-november-2010-mario-testino.

New York Times. "'Get Smart' Then and Now," September 19, 2011. www.nytimes.com/interactive/2008/06/15/movies/20080615_GETSMART_FEATURE.html?ref=annehathaway#.

Vanity Fair. "Behind the Scenes: Anne Hathaway on the Hollywood Issue Cover Shoot." Video, February 2, 2011. www.vanityfair.com/video/2011/02/773703088001.

Websites

Alluring Smile (www.annehathawayweb.com). This fan site dedicated to Anne Hathaway contains a biography, news, a press library, a fans lounge, and links to several sites that feature an Anne doll viewers can dress up.

Anne Hathaway Wedding (www.annehathawaywedding.com). This contains information on the nuptials of Anne Hathaway and Adam Shulman.

Get Real **Fan Club** (http://web.archive.org/web/20021016233849/http://getreal.anne-hathaway.com/main.html). This is the fan club site for the 1999–2000 TV series *Get Real* in which Anne Hathaway costarred as a teen.

Vassar College (www.vassar.edu). Vassar College, where Anne Hathaway studied for several years, is one of the premier liberal arts colleges in the United States. Its website offers information about courses of study and profiles of other famous alums, which include Noah Baumbach, Elizabeth Bishop, Sam Endicott, Marguarite Moreau, Lisa Kudrow, Justin Long, Edna St. Vincent Millay, Meryl Streep, Haley Taylor, Marc Thiessen, and Ethan Zohn.

About the Author

Cherese Cartlidge holds a bachelor's degree in psychology and a master's degree in education. She has published numerous books for children and young adults, including biographies of Neil Patrick Harris, Prince Harry, Beyoncé Knowles, and Jennifer Lopez. Cartlidge lives in Georgia with her two children.